HITLER'S OCCUPATION
OF UKRAINE (1941-1944)

A Study of Totalitarian Imperialism

by

Ihor Kamenetsky

The Marquette University Press

Marquette Slavic Studies are published under the direction of the Slavic Institute of Marquette University.

Edited by   Roman Smal-Stocki

Advisory Board   Alfred Sokolnicki
                    Christopher Spalatin

The views expressed in the Marquette Slavic Studies are those of their authors, and are not to be construed as representing the point of view of the Slavic Institute.

Library of Congress Catalog Card Number: 56-12215

Copyright, 1956, Marquette University Press, Milwaukee, Wis.

Contents

Acknowledgments

The writer is grateful to Dr. Robert G. Waite, professor of history at Williams College, Mass., for valuable advice and information.

The helpful guidance and assistance of Dr. Royden Dangerfield, professor of political science and director of the Institute of Government and Public Affairs at the University of Illinois, was especially appreciated.

The writer also is deeply obliged to the University of Illinois which provided him with basic sources for this work and to Stanford University and the Hoover Institute and Library on War and Revolution for access to rare and important documents.

Thanks is also given to Professor Witold Sworakowski of the Hoover Library for his kind help in locating the necessary materials for this book.

Gratitude is due Mrs. Edith Carrier and Mrs. Barbara Wittenstrom for helping with many details of preparing the manuscript for publication and to Mr. Yaroslav Terlecky for his kindness.

The author thanks the following publishers and authors for giving permission to quote from their publications:

American Book Co.: *The Great Powers and Eastern Europe* by John A. Lukacs (1953).

Curtis Publishing Co.: *Can Russia Trust Her Slave Armies* by Charles W. Thayer (1945).

Dial Press, Inc.: *A Guide to the Soviet Union* by William Mandel (1946).

Doubleday & Co., Inc.: *The Goebels Diaries*, trans. by Louis P. Lochner (1948, the Fireside Press, Inc.; reprinted by permission of Doubleday & Co., Inc.).

E. P. Dutton & Co., Inc.: *Panzer Leader* by Heinz Guderian (1952) and *Memoirs* by Franz von Papen (1953).

Foreign Affairs: *The Ideological Combat* by G. T. Robinson (1949).

Harvard University Press: *Terror and Progress USSR* by B. Moore, Jr. (1954).

Henry Holt and Co., Inc.: *The Political Economy of American Foreign Policy* by William Y. Elliot and others (1955).

Houghton Mifflin Co.: *Mein Kampf* by Adolf Hitler, translation of Ralph Manheim (1943).

Infantry Journal Press (now Combat Forces Press): *The World at War, 1939-1944,* (1944).

International Publishers: *Documents and Materials Relating to the Eve of the Second World War, Dirksen Papers, 1939-1939,* (1948).

The Macmillan Co.: *My Life in the Red Army* by Fred Virski (1949).

Sheed and Ward: *Europe and the German Question* by Friedrich W. Foerster (1940) and *The Inhuman Land* by Joseph Czapski (1952).

Edgar Snow: *The Ukraine Pays the Bill* (1945).

Ukrainian Book Club, editor Ivan Tyktor, Winnipeg, Canada: *History of the Ukrainian Armed Forces* by Ivan Krypyakevych and others (1953).

Introduction

Ukraine is a God-endowed country. For centuries she has excited the envy of her neighbors because of her unique situation, her fertile soil, her abundance of raw materials, and her gentle climate; and for centuries they have striven to absorb her.

Nor is Ukraine small. Within the Soviet Union alone her territory is between three and four times the size of Great Britain.[1]

Ukraine . . . in 1940 . . . was second only to the United States in the mining of iron, and dug twice as much as France, the leading European producer. Its blast furnaces smelted more pig iron than England and twice as much as France, being exceeded only by the United States and Germany. In steel production it stood fourth in the world, far ahead of such countries as France and Japan. Coal mining stood in the same position. . . . In field husbandry Ukraine is famous for more than its grain. Its potato crop is exceeded in the world only by Germany and Poland. It is the world's largest producer of beet-sugar. . . . Vegetable oil is pressed from an annual crop of more than a million tons of sunflower seed. Cotton and natural rubber from the roots of the dandelion-like koksagyz plant, are large new crops.[2]

This whole titanic struggle, which some are apt to dismiss as the "Russian glory," has in all truth and in many costly ways, been first of all a Ukrainian war. And the greatest of this republic's sacrifices, one which can be assessed in no ordinary ledger, is the toll taken of human life. No fewer than 10,000,000 people . . . have been 'lost' to Ukraine since the beginning of the war . . . No single European country has suffered deeper wounds to its cities, its industry, its farmlands and its humanity.[3]

THE OCCUPATION OF UKRAINE in the years 1941-1944 was not the first that country had to endure. Some of the earlier occupations lasted for hundreds of years, but they failed to attract the attention of the world. The German occupation, which lasted about three years, was one of the shortest and the

[1] Lancelot Lawton, "The Oppressed Ukrainians," *The Fortnightly Review* (April, 1934).
[2] William M. Mandel, *A Guide to the Soviet Union*, pp. 29-30.
[3] Edgar Snow, "The Ukraine Pays the Bill," *Saturday Evening Post* (Jan. 27, 1945).

most stirring. For Ukraine, this occupation brought the heaviest losses in human life and property in her history. For the world as a whole, the German ambitions toward Ukraine had most important implications. Ukraine, due to its size, fertility, and richness in the raw materials, was the most important goal of Hitler's expansion policy in Eastern Europe. To conquer and secure this area was an essential part of Hitler's *Lebensraum* theory. To achieve his ultimate goals in Eastern Europe, Hitler was not only ready to go to war with Poland, but also with Great Britain and France and finally with the Soviet Union. The conquest and colonization of Ukraine was one of Hitler's principal objectives and one of the major factors leading to the Second World War. Under German occupation, Ukraine became an experimental area where the Nazi theory of a superior race, mass extermination of the "subhuman" races, and preparation for the German settlement on a large scale were given full test. The Nazi occupation violated not only the basic provisions of the Hague Convention but also the rudimentary laws of humanity which had been accepted by Western society for centuries.

This study is concerned with the character and procedure of the Nazi occupation of Ukraine. It includes an investigation of the background and circumstances, explaining the temporary success of the German program and the reasons for its ultimate downfall. It is hoped that this study will reveal the more important aspects of the German occupation and will lead to a better understanding of the failure of German Eastern European politics during World War II. ·

CHAPTER 1

THE IDEOLOGICAL AND POLITICAL BACKGROUND OF THE OCCUPATION

There is no single item in Mein Kampf or in the glosses upon Mein Kampf, which has not a long history in Germany.[1]

One has also to take into consideration the fact that the activistic cynicism of totalitarianism is prepared by the fatigued cynicism of modern democracies, which are dominated by scepticism and relativism. The statesmen of the democracies no longer imagine that anyone takes seriously his own program. One read Hitler's "Mein Kampf" and was surprised as Hitler started to realize his aims.[2]

Hitler's Lebensraum Theory

THE KEY to understanding of German policy in Ukraine can be found in Hitler's single and basic work *Mein Kampf*. This work stresses three basic ideas of future German occupation policy. The first comes from the belief that the Slavs are an inferior race. The second is the knowledge that Eastern Europe, and especially Ukraine, was an ideal place for German agricultural colonization. The third proposition was that the most effective and most lasting way for expansion of a nation is physical force and conquest.

The ideas expressed by Hitler were by no means new nor are they confined to German thought. A look back to Hitler's predecessors will find much similarity in their ideas to those of Hitler. From the statement, "Force creates right; war is natural law,"[3] which was made by Otto von Bismarck who said he had built an empire of "blood and iron," a comparison can be drawn to a passage from *Mein Kampf*:

[1] W. W. Coole and M. F. Potter, *Thus Spake Germany*, (New York. Harper & Bros , 1941), p. 35.
[2] Waldemar Gurian, "The Philosophy of the Totalitarian State," in Charles Hart, *Philosophy of the State*, (Washington: G. Dawe, 1940), p. 62.
[3] Coole and Potter, *op. cit.*, p. 52.

1

. . . What is refused to amicable methods, it is up to the first to take. If our forefathers had let their decisions depend on the same pacifistic nonsense as our contemporaries, we should possess only a third of our present territory; but in that case there would be scarcely any German people for us to worry about in Europe today.[4]

As it existed a century ago, the German attitude regarding the Slavs may be perceived in the following paraphrase of a statement of Emperor William I in his reference to Poles:

The German nation was throughout permeated with the idea that its mission was to foist Teutonic ideals and Teutonic culture upon a people who were considered vastly inferior in every attribute that makes a nation great.[5]

The doctrine of the superiority of the German race was preached long before World War I by various Pan-Germanic organizations having differing ideologies. Especially interesting is a pamphlet published in 1900 by one such organization. This pamphlet envisaged formation of a gigantic German Empire by 1950, and the position of the German race in this Empire is described as follows:

Without doubt the Germans alone will not people the new German Empire thus constituted; but they alone will govern; they alone will exercise all political rights; they will serve in the navy and army; they alone will be able to acquire land. They will thus have, as in the Middle Ages, the sentiment of being a race of masters; nevertheless they will so far condescend that the less important work shall be done by the foreigners under their domination.[6]

A comparison of Hitler's comments in *Mein Kampf* with the above quoted passage, shows a close similarity of spirit:

For the organization of a Russian state formation was not the result of the political abilities of the Slavs in Russia, but only a wonderful example of the state-forming efficacity of the German element in an inferior race.[7]

---

[4] Adolf Hitler, *Mein Kampf,* trans. by R. Manheim, (New York: Literary Classics, Inc., 1942), p. 139.
[5] Otto Richard Tannenberg, *Grossdeutschland-die Arbeit des 20ten Jahrhunderts.* (Leipzig-Cohlis: B. Volger, 1911), p. 287.
[6] *Great Germany and Central Europe in the Year 1950* (pamphlet); quoted in Percy Evans Lewin, *The German Road to the East,* (London: William Heineman, 1917), pp. 12-13.
[7] Adolf Hitler, *op. cit.,* p. 654.

In the past 100 years, Otto von Bismarck was the first to push German expansion toward Eastern Europe, having promoted a forceful and intensive colonization in the part of Poland which belonged to Prussia. The idea of gaining for Germany some living space in Eastern Europe went farther than Poland itself. In 1881, the leading German Pan-Germanist, Paul de Legarde, wrote:

> . . . it is necessary to create a Central European Power which will guarantee the peace of all the Continent from the time when the Russians and Southern Slavs are cleared from the Black Sea, and when we shall have conquered for German colonization large territories to the east of our present frontiers.[8]

Prior to Hitler, the most recent attempt of the Germans to establish themselves in Ukraine was that of the German statesmen, Winkler and Lindequest, who attempted to create a German racial colony on the Crimean Peninsula during the German occupation of Ukraine in 1918. Enlightening regarding this is a letter written by a member of a German political mission in Kiev, Dr. Paul Rohrbach:

> I wanted to give Crimea and the Black Sea fleet to Ukraine, and I fought against Winkler's and Lindequist's idea of establishing a German racial colony in Cherson and Taurien.[9]

The above passage reflects an idea similar to that expressed by Hitler 25 years later when he fixed the policy to be followed in conquered Eastern Europe. In the conference with the high ranking individuals of the Third Reich on July 16, 1941, he said:

> Crimea must be cleared of all foreigners and settled by Germans. In the same way the old-Austrian Galizien will become a 'Reichsgebiet.'[10]

As can be seen, Hitler's ideas were not without historical origin and they were not his alone. They originated in the past and were promoted by Hitler's predecessors. They found

[8] Quoted by Paul de Lagarde in *Deutsche Schriften*, (1905), p 83, quoted in Lewin, *op cit*, p 318
[9] N. C Meyer, "Germans in the Ukraine, 1918," *The American Slavic and East European Review*, Vol. IX, No. 2, (April, 1950).
[10] International Military Tribunal, *Trial of the Major War Criminals*, Nuremberg, Secretariat of the Tribunal, 1947, Doc 221-L (hereafter cited as *Trials of War Criminals*).

a responsive audience within the German nation. Hitler had only to put the diverse ideas together, widen their scope, and set them down as one of the primary goals of Germany.[11] The goal of a new German expansion was expressed in *Mein Kampf* as follows:

> . . . . We National Socialists consciously draw a line beneath the foreign policy tendency of our pre-War period. We take up where we broke off six hundred years ago. We stop the endless German movement to the south and west, and turn our gaze toward the land in the east. At long last we break off the colonial and commercial policy of the pre-War period and shift to the soil policy of the future. If we speak of soil in Europe today, we can primarily have in mind only Russia and her vassal border states.[12]

A new idea which Hitler brought forth on behalf of a future German empire was that the core of the German nation should be the German peasant class. In this connection he differed from Bismarck and especially from Wilhelm II, both of whom supported the German industrial and business classes in their world trade and colonial ventures.

Hitler despised the cosmopolitan cities and the need of the Nation to depend on the commerce of other countries for livelihood. He pointed to the big cities as places of sterility, effeminity, and degeneration. He saw world trade as a promoter of cosmopolitanism which undermines the strength and identity of a nation. The peasants he viewed as the best and the healthiest element in preserving a great nation. Characteristics of the peasants such as conservatism, fertility, attachment to the land and the stubbornness with which they tried to get good results from poor German soil appealed to Hitler and were factors which led him to plan the Third Reich in terms of their interests. He exalted the importance of the German peasant class in the following words:

> . . . The possibility of preserving a healthy peasant class as a foundation for a whole nation can never be valued highly enough. Many of our present-day sufferings are only the consequence of the unhealthy relationship between rural and city population. A solid stock of low and middle class peasants has at all times been the best de-

[11] Adolf Hitler, *op. cit.*, p. 649.
[12] *Ibid.*, p. 654.

fense against social ills such as we possess today. And, moreover, this is the only solution which enables a nation to earn its daily bread within the inner circuit of its economy. Industry and commerce recede from their unhealthy leading position and adjust themselves to the general framework of a national economy of balanced supply and demand.[13]

Hitler realized that, although Germany possessed considerable industrial facilities, she did not possess enough good soil. To make German peasants the core of the nation and to provide the German population with sufficient food required land resources Germany did not possess. Acquisition of land was inevitable if German peasants were to become of vital importance to the Nation and if Germany was to become self sufficient in food production. One solution for the need of additional territory would be the regaining of German colonies in Africa where some German farmer colonies had been established before the first World War. Hitler rejected this possibility:

For it is not in colonial acquisitions that we must see the solution of this problem, but exclusively in the acquisition of a territory for settlement, which will enhance the area of the mother country, and hence not only keep the new settlers in the most intimate community with the land of their origin, but secure for the total area those advantages which lie in its unified magnitude.[14]

When Hitler ruled out the acquisition of colonial territories as a solution, Europe was the only possible place where Germany could expand. And Hitler did not leave the world in doubt concerning the area of future German expansion. He said:

If land was desired in Europe, it could be obtained by and large only at the expense of Russia, and this meant that the new Reich must again set itself on the march along the road of the Teutonic Knights of old, to obtain by the German sword sod for the German plow and daily bread for the nation.[15]

There was one question unanswered in Hitler's scheme. What was to happen to the population in the areas which Hitler

---

[13] *Ibid.*, p. 138.
[14] *Ibid*, p. 653.
[15] *Ibid*, p. 140.

marked for German colonization? The Fuehrer gave no direct
answer in his book. His reference to the imitation of the order
of Teutonic Knights, who completely eliminated the original
Baltic inhabitants of East Prussia, was at least an admonishing
hint. Hitler held faithfully to the main objectives outlined in his
book. It was, on the whole, not only a blueprint of his intentions but also of his actions. Although this book was printed
in 1925 and was widely circulated in Germany and other countries following Hitler's coming to power, it was never taken
very seriously. It was quite late before the nations concerned
and the leading powers seriously considered his outline for
conquest. A social psychologist may be more qualified to explain
this strange lack of reaction, but part of the answer is given by
Machiavelli:

> But men are so simple, and governed so much by their
> present needs, that he who wishes to deceive will never
> fail in finding willing dupes.[16]

How Hitler Opened the Road to the East

At the time Hitler took over, Germany was emerging from
the status of a defeated power. It is difficult to understand how
Germany could regain its old political and military strength
while conducting a vigorous aggressive policy. Having lost
World War I, she was without an army, had lost her colonies
and considerable parts of the Motherland, could not rearm, was
surrounded by hostile neighbors and was watched constantly by
the Allies.

If we carefully analyze the reasons for the phenomenal
success of Hitler's politics, we find two factors which contributed
to it: a) the threat of Communism; b) the principle of self-
determination.

We can hardly deny that Hitler's dynamic attack against
Communism was acceptable to most European states, especially
to the two leading European powers—England and France. The
activity in the Third International gave rise to many tensions
after World War I and even caused a temporary break of diplomatic relations between Great Britain and the Soviet Union.
The existence of millions of Communists in Germany and the
shadow of world revolution spread fear and distrust in many

[16] Niccolo Machiavelli, *The Prince,* trans by N. H. Thomson, (Oxford.
Clarendon Press, 1917), p. 127.

European states. This feeling of fear and insecurity was strengthened and aggravated by the realization that there was no effective force which could stop Russia if she should decide to march
westward. Because neither Poland, Rumania, nor the Baltic
states could be counted upon as an effective barrier and because
the League of Nations showed an apparent weakness as an
instrument against aggression, a dynamic and militantly anti-
Communistic Germany seemed to be an effective counterpoise
to a militantly anti-Capitalistic Soviet Union.

Though the danger of Communist aggression in 1933 did not
appear as great as it does today, it was significant enough for the
Western powers not to interfere actively with Hitler's rearming
of Germany. Some influential circles in Great Britain viewed a
rearmed Germany as a barricade against Soviet penetration in
Central Europe. The views of some groups in England are reflected in the reports of the NSDAP[17] Office for Foreign Affairs
of October, 1935:

> The British paper, *The Aeroplane,* published by the
> Air Force staff attacked Bolshevism sharply, as usual, it
> attacked the campaign hostile to German rearmament
> and stated that a Germany possessing a strong Air Force
> and ready to strike against the Asiatic barbarians, would
> be welcome.[18]

Such prominent personalities of the British political world
as Mr. Hoare, then Minister of Foreign Affairs in Great Britain,
showed an interest in the Nazi movement. The above document
continues:

> On his (Hoare's) request he was given a memoran-
> dum prepared by us concerning the spiritual principles of
> National Socialism. He opinionized that he will try to
> better understand our movement.[19]

It is also known that Sir Henry Deterding, English oil mag-
nate, and the Marquis of Londonberry, author of the book
Ourselves and Germany, showed attitudes friendly to Nazi Germany. They were motivated by an antagonism to Communism.[20]

[17] NSDAP—National Sozialistische Deutsche Arbeiter Partei, the official
name of National-Socialistic Party.
[18] Trials of War Criminals, *op. cit*, Doc. 003-PS.
[19] *Ibid*, Doc 003-PS.
[20] The Marquis of Londonderry gave his motives for Anglo-German cooperation in the following terms.

Fear of Soviet Russia motivated Poland to conclude a ten-year non-aggression pact with Germany. Germany, through its anti-Communist pact, gained Italy and Japan as allies. Germany was thus able to overcome the two stumbling blocks of military impotency and political isolation on its way toward the East.

Still another factor gave Hitler opportunity to implement his expansion policy. This was the principle of the self-determination of nations which Hitler used first to annex German irredenta and then to support other independence movements. It was hard to deny Hitler the right of self-determination because it was the principle which the Western Allies themselves professed during World War I. It was included in the covenant of the League of Nations, which they had sponsored. German claims, based on the principle of self-determination, found a warm response in Great Britain. Great Britain was known not only as a champion of the rights of nationalities in the 19th century, but also conducted a liberal policy toward other nationalities. In accordance with this liberal policy, she had granted independence to Ireland and Iraq in the Statute of Westminister and had granted independence within the Commonwealth to her dominions. How deeply the principle of self-determination was rooted in English public opinion at the time may be indicated by a statement of a member of British Parliament who said during the Sudeten German crisis:

> You can hardly expect us, who in every part of the globe have stood for national self-determination, even for Ireland, where it was particularly difficult for us and seemed so dangerous, to oppose self-determination for the Sudeten Germans.[21]

Hitler's success in getting the Sudetenland after the signing of the Treaty of Munich was not his only achievement at this time. In the same Treaty, other minorities in Czechoslovakia—Slovaks and Carpatho-Ukrainians—were given a broad autonomy within the state, and Hitler was the person who was credited for it. Hitler acted like a champion of self-determination not only for the German nation but also for all the peoples who

I was at a loss to understand why we could not make common ground in some terms or other with Germany in opposition to Communism . . . . The anti-Communism platform was (and still is) invaluable   (The Marquis of Londonderry, *Ourselves and Germany*, R. Hall, Ltd , 1938, p. 129)

[21] Friedrich W. Foerster, *Europe and the German Question*, (New York: Sheed & Ward, 1940), p. 379.

felt themselves oppressed. These circumstances were used by Hitler in justifying expansion toward Eastern Europe.

The area in Eastern Europe most desired by Hitler was Ukraine. The American consul in Berlin, Raymond H. Geist, recalls that he had a conversation with the German chief of staff in December, 1938, who mentioned that German expansion toward the East was inevitable and that Ukraine was particularly important.[22] Ukraine, with its fertile black soil, seemed to Hitler to be the best area for German agricultural colonization.

To conceal her colonial plans, Germany acted as a champion of an independent Ukrainian state. In the autumn of 1938, the German radio station in Vienna started to transmit special broadcasts to Ukrainians in the Soviet Ukraine and in Western Ukraine which was under Poland. The Ukrainian national spirit in the autonomous Carpatho-Ukraine was encouraged. It was generally assumed in the political circles in the West that Carpatho-Ukraine would become the nucleus for the future great Ukrainian state.

Ukrainian nationalism and the Ukrainian striving for independence were potentially strong factors contributing to political realignment in Eastern Europe. Ukrainian nationalism had been important at the time of the Russian Revolution in 1917. An autonomous and then fully independent republic was organized, and it managed to maintain its independence until 1920 when it succumbed to superior forces of Poles and Red and White Russians. After World War I, Ukrainian unrest continued. In 1930, the Soviet government uncovered in Ukraine a "Union for the Liberation of the Ukraine," and 45 leading Ukrainian scholars and scientists were tried for allegiance to it in a spectacular trial in Kharkhiv.[23] From then on, the charges were common that a Ukrainian "bourgeois nationalism" existed. The nationalist movement included such personalities as Chubar, head of the Ukrainian Soviet government from 1925 to 1933, and his successor, Lubchenko, 1933-1937, and Minister of Education Skrypnyk. All leaders of the movement were liquidated or committed suicide.

In late autumn of 1938 and the early part of 1939, the psychological and political situation seemed most favorable for the German march toward Ukraine. There were two major factors

---

[22] *Trials of War Criminals, op. cit.,* Doc. 1759-PS
[23] *Encyclopedia of Ukraine,* (New York-Munich: Shevchenko Scientific Society, 1949), pp. 545-578.

to be considered. One of them was that Poland and Rumania, which blocked Hitler's way to the East, were not strongly determined to resist Hitler's march against the Soviet Union. Their relations with the Soviet Union were never very friendly, and the Polish-German Non-aggression Pact of 1934 and the Polish-Rumanian Common Defense Pact of 1931, which was valid at the end of 1938, were definitely directed against the Red Colossus.[24]

The prospect of having a Ukrainian buffer state on their eastern boundaries (with about 30 million population) instead of a Red Giant with 180 millions must have been welcome to Poland and Rumania, although both of them controlled regions of Ukraine.

Such a possibility must have represented a special inducement for Poland, especially when Germany tried to awaken the old Polish ambitions toward Soviet Ukraine by offering a partnership in a common action against the Soviet Union.[25] The Polish interest in this direction as well as the vacillating attitude of Polish rulers to these German proposals is reflected in a memorandum of Foreign Minister Ribbentrop dated Jan. 9, 1939, concerning a conversation with Polish Foreign Minister Beck in Munich on Jan. 6, 1939:

> I asked Beck whether they had given up Marshal
> Pilsudski's aspirations in this direction, that is, toward the

---

[24] *Ibid.*

[25] At this time, Warsaw was one of the centers of the Ukrainian National Republic government-in-exile (UNR). The UNR government claimed its authority from the revolutionary Ukrainian parliament, Central Rada, and descended directly from the Directory government headed by Symon Petlura in 1919 The UNR government signed a mutual assistance treaty with Poland in 1920, and shortly afterward, the Polish and the Ukrainian Republican troops started the well-known "March on Kiev." Kiev was then under Soviet occupation.

At this point, the venture proved unsuccessful, the Polish government signed a peace treaty in Riga in which it recognized the Soviet Ukrainian government and withdrew formal recognition of the UNR government Nevertheless, the Polish government regarded it as useful to support informally the Ukrainian exile government in Paris, hoping that the "March on Kiev" could be repeated in case of internal difficulties in the Soviet Union Thus, several ministers of UNR were employed in the Warsaw Ukrainian Institute, sponsored by the Polish government, and nearly 100 former officers of UNR army were commissioned in the Polish army.

In the eventful days of 1938-1939, the Ukrainian exile government gained significance. It conducted a lively two-way diplomatic game The president of UNR, Andrew Livytskyi, tried to protect the Ukrainian interests in Polish-German bargainings in Warsaw; at the same time, the Foreign Minister of UNR Alexander Shulhyn, tried to gain support of the Western Allies for the Ukrainian cause in Paris.

Ukraine, he answered that they had even been in Kiev, and that these aspirations were doubtless still alive to-day.[26]

Another memorandum by Ribbentrop after a conversation with Beck in Warsaw on Jan. 26, 1939, reflects the same atti-tude:

> I then spoke to Minister Beck once more about the policy to be pursued by Poland and Germany toward the Soviet Union and in this connection also spoke about the question of the Greater Ukraine and again proposed German-Polish cooperation in this field.
>
> Minister Beck made no secret of the fact that Poland had aspirations directed toward the Soviet Ukraine and a connection at the Black Sea; but at the same time he called attention to the supposed dangers to Poland that in the Polish view arise from the treaty with Germany directed against the Soviet Union.[27]

Rumanian King Carol, who visited Germany by the end of November, 1938, accepted the German idea about the creation of a Greater Ukraine at the expense of the Soviet Union as a matter of course and only expressed his concern about the status of the Rumanian eastern boundaries.[28] King Carol's visit to Germany was followed in December by closer ties embodied in the trade treaty between Germany and Rumania. This action indicated that Rumania was not much concerned about the pending German march against the Soviet Union which could require a transit through Rumanian territory.

A second important factor which favored a German march against the Soviet Union at this time was the attitude of Great Britain. Great Britain was inclined to believe that the British interests and safety would be best served when Ukraine was independent from Russia. Here again the principle of self-deter-mination was important in crystallizing British sentiments. Per-haps the principle of self-determination was substantiated by the sad experience of the British in her intervention in the Russian Civil War. In this war, Great Britain supported a "Holy and Undivided Russia" and failed. Soviet Russia then claimed and won the right of self-determination for the nations of the old

[26] *Documents on German Foreign Policy*, 1918-1945, (U.S Printing Office, Washington, 1953), Series D, V, 161
[27] *Ibid.*, p. 168.
[28] *Ibid.*, p 345.

Russian empire. Perhaps economic interests and the idea of an effective *cordon sanitaire* against Communism were equally important in shaping British policy. At any rate, there is evidence that such sentiment existed in British political circles between the World Wars. Enlightening, in this connection, is a passage taken from the Diary of Viscount d'Abernon:

> Berlin, Aug. 30, 1922: . . ., even as regards the Black Sea and the Mediterranean, a Russia divided into different States, whose commercial interests overpowered her political ambition would make our position far more secure in the event of the re-establishment of a powerful Empire. A separatist policy for Ukraine would unquestionably lead to a safer and more healthy position in the Black Sea, and would facilitate commercial control of the Straits, as opposed to political control.[29]

It is obvious that Great Britain never considered direct military or diplomatic measures for an Eastern European realignment. Neither her strategic position nor English public opinion would favor direct British entanglement in the Eastern European affairs. But the emergence of a militant and anti-Communist Nazi Germany, with considerable economic and military resources and with a program of *Drang nach Osten,* offered possibility to achieve such rearrangement with no effort and at little expense. It is interesting to notice that such a possibility was considered in Great Britain one year after Hitler came to power. A leading British journalist, Lancelot Lawton, wrote in an article in 1934:

> Whereas formerly German statesmen looked both to the East and to the West, Hitler at present looks to the East only. . . . No one who studies the map of eastern Europe can doubt that there are immense possibilities of German-Polish compromise at the expense of others. The idea of including Ukraine within the Western European system, and moving Russia on toward the East is certainly tempting. . . .

> An independent or autonomous Ukraine is indispensable for European economic progress and for world peace. Through Ukraine lies the shortest land route from the West to Persia and India. Were she to achieve self-government it would mean the end of Russia's Byzantine dreams and Indian longings. . . .

[29] *Daily Herald,* quoted from W. P. and Zelda K. Coates, *History of Anglo-Soviet Relations,* (London: Lawrence and Wishhart, 1944), pp. 329-30.

With Ukraine as a part of a democratic federated system there would, it is hoped, come into existence a grouping of States with which Great Britain could be on friendly terms. The moment is long overdue for the creation of some such grouping in Eastern Europe.[30]

A report by the German ambassador in London shows how far public opinion had crystallized on behalf of an Independent Ukraine at the time when Hitler had the means for realization of this idea. Ambassador Dirksen wrote from London on Jan. 4, 1939:

If a Ukrainian state were to come into being with German help, even if it were of military nature, under the psychologically skillful slogan, freely circulated by Germany: 'Self-determination for the Ukrainians, liberation of Ukraine from the domination of Bolshevist Jewry' this would be accepted here by British public opinion, especially if consideration for British economic interests in the development of the new state were an added inducement for the British. Britain would never allow a conflict to arise over the realization of the right of self-determination.[31]

It is shown in the same Dirksen report that a conflict between the Soviet Union and Poland, which might arise during a German march toward Ukraine, was not of particular concern to the British public:

In all discussions on the situation of Poland and the Soviet Union there can be noted in the British press a fundamentally different attitude from that adopted toward the Czech question. Whereas in the latter question the British press from the start took the view that Britain could not disinterest herself in the fate of Czechoslovakia, such statements with regard to Poland and the Soviet Union are now entirely lacking.[32]

British public opinion was not opposed in principle to Hitler's liberation of Ukraine. What really mattered was the German aim there and what would be the effect on the balance of power in Europe. If Hitler's aim in Ukraine were purely of economic nature and similar to that which Great Britain pursued

---

[30] Lancelot Lawton, "The Oppressed Ukrainians," *The Fortnightly Review,* (April, 1934).
[31] *Documents on German Foreign Policy, op cit.,* IV, 367.
[32] *Ibid.,* p. 366.

in her dominions or which the U.S.A. followed in some smaller
Latin American states, then the possibility of a complete understanding existed. If, however, Hitler planned to create a Greater
Germany in the East instead of a Greater Ukraine, England
would be forced to prevent it by all means, including a war.[33]
The latter goal of German expansion would not only violate the
principle of self-determination but would also upset completely
the balance of power in Europe. A Germany with boundaries
stretching from the Rhine to the Caucasus Mountains would
certainly present a greater danger of hegemony in Europe than
did the Soviet Union with her boundaries of 1939. The pressure
by Great Britain for clarification of German plans in Eastern
Europe, when the German action in this direction seemed imminent, is again reflected in Dirksen's report from London on
Jan. 3, 1939:

> . . . a further German penetration toward Ukraine, whose
> conquest by Germany is firmly believed in Great Britain
> to be timed for the spring of 1939, would be accepted
> . . . . There is, however, a wish to learn what Germany's
> aims are and a desire for negotiations with Germany by
> which to achieve clarification and pacification of the
> world   political   situation,   delimination   of   spheres   of
> interest, and economic agreement.[34]

It can be seen in von Papen's *Memoirs* that Dirksen was
right in his evaluation of Anglo-Saxon sentiment and that the
idea of an independent Ukraine bound economically to Germany
persisted even during the war. Describing his secret negotiations with the representatives of the Western Allies, von Papen
mentions one of their proposals:

[33] Speech of Lord Halifax two months before the outbreak of World War II.
    Every developed community is faced with the vital problem of
    living space But the problem is not solved simply by acquiring
    more territory that may indeed only make the problem more
    acute It can only be solved by wise ordering of the affairs of
    a country at home, and by adjusting its relation with the other
    countries abroad. Nations expand their wealth, and raise the
    standard of living of their people, by gaining the confidence of
    their neighbours, and thus facilitating the flow of goods between
    them The very opposite is likely to be the consequence of action
    by one nation in suppression of the independence of her smaller
    and weaker 'neighbours. And if *Lebensraum* is to be applied in
    that sense, we reject it and must resist its application. Through
    cooperation—and we for our part, are ready to cooperate—there
    is ample scope for extending to all these means, which are implied
    in the term *Lebensraum* Cf Hans W Weigert, *Generals and
    Geographers,* (London: Oxford University Press, 1942), p. 221.
[34] *Documents on German Foreign Policy, op. cit.,* IV, 362.

The former frontiers were to be restored in the West, and Poland must be assured of an independent existence in the East. The film also said that the Allies realized Germany was not self-sufficient, and therefore suggested that Ukraine should be made an independent state, though associated somehow or other with Germany.[35]

Clarification of Hitler's aims in his *Drang nach Osten* came in a drastic form on March 15, 1939, when Germany occupied Bohemia and Moravia and gave Carpatho-Ukraine to Hungary. The clarification was in the spirit of *Mein Kampf* but certainly was not the action expected by Great Britain. The British were relying on Hitler's recent tirades endorsing self-determination. The importance of Hitler's actions on English attitudes toward Germany is characterized by Dirksen as follows:

> . . . .The German march into Bohemia and Moravia, and the occupation of Prague, marked a turning point in Anglo-American relations and in Britain's foreign policy generally.[36]

Hitler's last annexation caused Great Britain to abandon hope of an understanding with Germany and to seriously consider the possibility of war. Two days after the German occupation of Bohemia and Moravia and the abandonment of Carpatho-Ukraine to Hungary, British Prime Minister Chamberlain said in his speech in Birmingham:

> Is this the last attack upon a small state or is it to be followed by others? Is this, in fact, a step in the direction of an effort to dominate the world by force? . . . I am not going to answer (these questions) tonight but I am sure that they will require grave and serious consideration. . . . While I am not prepared to engage this country by new and unspecified commitments operating under conditions which cannot now be foreseen yet no greater mistake could be made than to suppose that because it believes war to be a senseless and cruel thing, this nation has so lost its fibre that it will not take part to the utmost of its power in resisting such a challenge if it ever were made.[37]

[35] Franz von Papen, *Memoirs,* (New York E P Dutton & Co., Inc , 1953), p 505

[36] *Documents and Materials Relating to the Eve of the Second World War,* Dirksen Papers, 1938-1939, (New York. International Publisher, 1948), II, p 167.

[37] Frederick L. Schuman, *International Politics,* 4th ed., (New York McGraw-Hill, 1948), pp. 843-844.

Great Britain started seriously to rearm for war. The rearmament program was accompanied by intensive diplomatic action. First, Great Britain made attempts to block Hitler's march toward the East. Poland was given an Anglo-French guarantee on March 31. Another was given to Rumania on April 13. Some attempts were made to bring the Soviet Union into the British scheme as early as March 18, but subsequent negotiations in these directions were clouded ·by the unwillingness of Poland and Rumania to consider the Soviet Union as their protector and guardian. But whatever new defensive plans Great Britain might have devised, they were bound to come late. Hitler, in planning the seizure of Prague, considered the worsening of relations with Great Britain and the possibility of an eventual war with the West. He saw that England was unwilling to give him a free hand in Europe, meanwhile concerning herself with her overseas empire as he suggested in *Mein Kampf*. Hitler realized also that he had to cease using the principle of self-determination sooner or later if he wanted to realize the plans set forth in *Mein Kampf*. Thus, if the break between Germany and Western Democracies was to come, Hitler preferred the break at a time when the West was militarily unprepared and weak. While proceeding with the occupation of Bohemia and Moravia, Hitler was preparing a new scheme to eliminate the influence of the Western Democracies on the European continent, and would then start an unhampered march towards his Eastern European "Garden of Eden." When he started his next annexation, Hitler planned to arrange a temporary truce with the Soviet Union in order to avoid a two-front war. Shortly after the occupation of Prague, he mentioned to General Brauchitsch, chief of staff of the German army: "My next step you would hardly expect." Jokingly he added, "Have a seat, please, I am going to make a formal visit in Moscow."[38]

Hitler's speech of April 28, 1939, contained none of the usual attacks against the Soviet Union. The German military attache in Moscow, General Koestring, tried to convince Japan to leave the Soviet Union alone and to turn against the Anglo-Saxons instead.[39] Appeasement by Germany of the Soviet Union was most successful. It was crowned with a non-aggression pact between these two states, signed on Aug. 23, 1939, in Moscow.

---

[38] Erich Kordt, *Wahn und Wirklichkeit* (Stuttgart: Union Deutsche Verlagsgesellschaft, 1948), p. 157.
[39] *Ibid.*

The Soviet Union in taking this step had objectives similar to those of Great Britain a half year earlier. While Great Britain wanted to use National Socialism as a hammer to crush Communism, playing advantageously the role of a happy third, the Soviet Union had the same designs in mind with respect to the Western Democracies and Germany. Hitler, however, was the party who attained the greatest immediate success. He temporarily eliminated the danger of a two-front war and won full cooperation of the Soviet Union in crushing Poland, the last stumbling block on the way toward Ukraine.

CHAPTER 2

ON THE EVE OF "ACTION BARBAROSSA"

A Nationalist Germany, under determined and clear-sighted leadership, would be in position to enter into an alliance even with the devil, although only for a limited period, and in that case alone would it be possible at least to consider a political arrangement with Soviet Russia.[1]

The decision about war against the Soviet Union was made much earlier than 1940. The fight against Bolshevism was such a basic nucleus of national-socialistic ideology that it would be a complete misapprehension to regard the Soviet treaty as a principal turn and not what it really was—a temporary maneuver for overcoming Poland.[2]

Why Did Hitler Decide on a Two-Front War in 1941?

THE GERMAN-RUSSIAN non-aggression pact signed in August, 1939, was a master stroke which surprised the world and allowed Hitler to start an assault on Poland two weeks later. Poland was overrun in three weeks, and a common boundary with the Soviet Union was established by the end of September.

The Soviet Union was eager to cooperate. German military records indicate that from the years 1939 to 1941 the Soviet Union supplied them regularly and sufficiently with foods and raw materials. The Russians even supplied Germany with important war materials, such as zinc and rubber, which Russia was able to obtain in England. From the summer of 1939 to June, 1941, Russian deliveries to Germany included 1,000,000 tons of grain, 500,000 tons of wheat, 900,000 tons of oil derivatives, 100,000 tons of cotton, 500,000 tons of phosphates, 10,000 tons of flax, 80 million Reichsmarks worth of lumber, and an un-

---

[1] Alfred Rosenberg, *Voelkischer Beobachter*, April 18, 1926.
[2] Peter Kleist, *Zwischen Hitler und Stalin, 1939-1945*, (Bonn. Athenaeum Verlag, 1950), p. 124.

specified amount of manganese and platinum.[3] Offers of Soviet aid included shelter and repair facilities for German submarines at Murmansk and Arkhangelsk and of the sale of a certain number of Soviet submarines to the Germans. The Germans rejected the offer of submarines for political reasons.[4]

Of no less importance was the fact that the Soviet Union, which participated with Germany in dividing some of the spoils in Europe, conducted a powerful propaganda campaign justifying Hitler's aggression and condemning the Western Allies as war criminals. In possession of the most effective propaganda channels and virtually in control of Communist organizations abroad, the Soviet Union contributed much to the German cause in foreign countries. Of course, the Soviet Union had her own plans in pursuing such a policy. With express or tacit German agreement, the Soviets took Western Ukraine and Byelo-Russia, the Baltic states, Bukovina, and Bessarabia and showed eagerness in extension of influence in the Balkans. But there were no serious misunderstandings about any territorial issues between the Soviet Union and Germany which could serve as a reason for a war between the two countries. There were several signs[5] that the Soviet Union was eager to avoid a war with Germany, not because of the inferiority of her arms but because of the unreliability of her citizens.[6]

Within a year after signing the non-aggression treaty with the Soviet Union, Hitler decided to discard it. Brilliant military successes had given him possession of Western and Northern Europe, and Hitler felt he was virtual ruler of the continent. England still remained to be fought and defeated. Sober military considerations seemed to suggest the ending of the Western war. Conquest of the Mediterranean area, Gibraltar, Suez canal, and a tight blockade against Great Britain could be achieved by the summer of 1940.[7] But Hitler's strategy proved many times to be dictated by his political visions and not by political or military realities. England had been driven off the Continent, and this was what Hitler wanted as far as Britain was concerned. Hitler had no particular ambitions in Western

---

[3] *Trials of War Criminals, Documentary Survey by Vice-Admiral Assman,* XXXIV, p. 674.

[4] *Ibid ,* p. 679

[5] John A. Lukacs, *The Great Powers and Eastern Europe,* (New York: American Book Co., 1953), p. 401.

[6] *Vide supra,* pages 32-33.

[7] Kurt von Tippelskirch, *Geschichte des Zweiten Weltkrieges,* (Bonn: Athenaeum Verlag, 1951), p. 113.

Europe, and in the light of his ideology, his peace offer to the West following the Polish and French campaigns seems to have reflected a genuine desire to finish the conflict in the West peacefully. But there still remained a magic goal in Eastern Europe for which Hitler had launched the war—the fertile plains of Ukraine, sunny Crimea, the subtropical Caucasus. In one, two, or at the most three months of German assault, the Soviet Union would be crushed. The conquest of the Continent could then be completed, and England would be forced to yield because she would never be able to wage a war on the Continent without the support of a continental nation. To bring Great Britain to its knees indirectly through the crushing of the Soviet Union was considered by Hitler to be his best stategy as can be seen from his letter to Mussolini of June 21, 1941, which reveals in part:

> The hopes of England rest on two principals: Russia and America. We have no chance to eliminate America. But we have enough power to annihilate Russia.[8]

If the Soviet Union were to be crushed, thought Hitler, England would yield, and valuable German blood would not be squandered upon foreign soil. Still he was ready to let the blood of his soldiers flow freely on the black soil of Ukraine because that soil was to become German. It is probable that Hitler reached his decision to attack the Soviet Union some time during July, 1940, and at that time gave his first orders to prepare for the campaign. There is evidence that the first steps to develop operational plans for the conquest of the Soviet Union were taken by the end of July, 1940.[9] Former German Field Marshal Paulus testified during the Nuremberg Trials that from September, 1940, when he joined the German general staff, he continued to develop "Action Barbarossa,"[10] which was finally completed early in November of 1940. At approximately the same time German troops were concentrated on the Soviet border. The German High Army Command stated on Aug. 27, 1940:

> The present forces in Poland are to be strengthened immediately . . . 10 infantry and 2 armored divisions to be transferred to south-eastern Poland to be ready in case of "intervention" in Rumania.[11]

[8] Kleist, *Zwischen Hitler und Stalin*, p 125
[9] Kurt von Tippelskirch, *op cit* , p 199
[10] *Trial of War Criminals*, XXII, 455.
[11] Lukacs, *op cit* , p 320.

And on Sept. 6 the German army received a directive from Abwehr (German counterintelligence) which was dated Aug. 26:

> The Eastern territory will be manned stronger in the weeks to come. . . . These regroupings must not create the impression in Russia that we are preparing an offensive in the East. . . . The impression is to be created that the center of the massing of troops is in the southern part of the General Government, in the Protectorate and in Austria and that the massing in the North is relatively unimportant.[12]

These facts concerning Hitler's preparations to attack the Soviet Union have another implication. They indicate that Hitler reached his decision far ahead of Molotov's visit to Berlin on Nov. 12, 1940. It is hardly tenable that Molotov's demands for an extension of Russian influence in the Balkans and Hitler's refusal were the cause of Hitler's preparations to annihilate the Soviet Union. In the absence of any serious diplomatic or military controversies between Germany and the Soviet Union in July, 1940, when Hitler's decision was reached, the only basis for that decision is to be found in advanced planning based upon Nazi ideology.

The Assault on the East and the German Political Conceptions

Preparations for the "Action Barbarossa" showed that not only military plans but a political program and an administrative plan had to be developed for Eastern areas which would be conquered in the future. Though his statements in *Mein Kampf* left little doubt about the real German purpose in Eastern Europe, even Hitler realized that this could not be given as a real excuse for declaring war. It was also clear that political propaganda or political measures would be necessary to prepare for the rapid disintegration of the Soviet Union and for an easier administration of the East. Yet, political-administrative preparations for the campaign started relatively late. The first preparatory work in this field began in April, 1941, although military preparations started in the summer of 1940.[13]

---

[12] *Ibid* , p. 320.
[13] On April 2, 1941, Hitler had ordered Rosenberg to organize a central political bureau for East-Work, which was the first attempt at political-administrative preparations (*Trial of War Criminals*, XXVI, 543)

Hitler made Alfred Rosenberg responsible for preparing the administrative scheme and the political line in the East, although, as shall be seen later, the methods which Rosenberg suggested were pushed aside by Hitler as impractical or superfluous. Rosenberg's personality and his political scheme for the East are interesting, not because he was regarded as the "best brain" among the Nazi theorists, but because he was the single man of the Nazi hierarchy who knew Old Russia and Russian problems. His ideas on racial theory and German aims did not differ at all from those of Hitler, but his methods followed the "Russian school," with its refined psychological warfare and the ability to take political advantages, in place of the rude Nazi use of sheer force, brutal physical intimidation or suppression.

Rosenberg's political and administrative policy was roughly as follows:

1.   He wanted to divide the Soviet Empire into five parts— Great Finland, Baltic protectorate, Ukrainian National state, Caucasian Federative state, and Russia proper.

2.   Finland was to be given, besides territory which she lost in the War of 1939-40, the territory of the Karelo-Finish Soviet-Republic and the District of Leningrad. Finland was to be built into a strong state, which was to be made a part of the German alliance system.

3.   The Baltic protectorate was to be composed of Lithuania, Latvia, Estonia, and Byelo-Russia, and was to remain under strict supervision of Germany. This administrative unit, which Rosenberg named "Ostland," was chosen as the first object of Germanization and colonization.

4.   Ukraine was to be created as an independent state, and the Ukrainian national spirit was to be promoted. Some ethnographically Russian provinces (Kursk, Saratov, Tambov, Voronesh) were to be included within the Ukrainian state to increase Ukrainian-Russian antagonism. The Ukrainian state would include a territory of 1.1 million square kilometers and 59.5 millions of people within its boundaries.[14] The Ukrainian state would also be the temporary base for German policy in the East and would serve as a shield against the restoration ambitions of Russia and as a cover for the German colonization in "Ostland."

[14] *Trials of War Criminals*, Doc. 1058-PS.

5. A Transcaucasian federative state would be formed from the Caucasian peoples, and Germany would control this state.

6. The rest of the Soviet Empire would form a Russian state, but its shape and character were to be determined later.

7. The independent states of Ukraine and Transcaucasia would possess their own government, but, as indicated by Rosenberg, these governments would be under the political supervision of a German Reichskommissar and under the military supervision of a German military governor.

Such was the "New Order" which Rosenberg designed for the occupied Soviet Union and communicated to "those most closely concerned with the Eastern problem" on June 20, 1941.[15] Rosenberg wanted Germany to take full political advantage, acting as a liberator of Soviet nations from Soviet Russian oppression. He suggested also that Germany should exercise simultaneously a political and military control in the "liberated areas" so as to be able to eliminate independence of the nations concerned at the proper time. Rosenberg's reasons for this policy may be seen in the following statement:

> A war for the purpose of establishing an undivided Russia is out of the question. . . . Russia was never a one-nation state. She was always a state of many nations. The Great Russian historians have tried for 150 years, and with great success, to present a picture to Western Europe of a Russia settled only by Russians, ruled only by Russians, as if she were a state created in the same manner as Germany, England or France. . . .[16]

The immediate conclusion of this reasoning is expressed by Rosenberg:

> The task of our policy seems to be the exploiting of the desire for liberty of all peoples (within the Soviet Union) and the crystallization of these strivings in a determined state form.[17]

There can be little doubt that Rosenberg's strategy was designed to achieve final German visionary goals in Eastern Europe. He said in the same speech: "We lead today not a 'Crusade against Bolshevism' for the sake of liberating the 'poor

---

[15] *Ibid*
[16] *Ibid*
[17] *Ibid.*

Russians' once and forever from Bolshevism, but with the purpose of pursuing German 'Welt Politik.' "[18]

It is obvious that the aims of Rosenberg were not altruistic. He did not intend to liberate the nations of the East, but he recognized them as a weakness of the Soviet Empire and wanted to utilize them for German ends.[19] He knew that the different nations within the Soviet Empire had been held down by brutal force, suppression, purge, terror, and deportations. He knew also from Russian history that most of these nations were successfully brought within the Russian Empire by alliances, federations, and successions which led to their semi-dependence on Russia and finally their national suppression. It is no wonder that Rosenberg, who had been educated in Old Russia, would emphasize the policy of promises, friendliness, and formal concessions as the most effective weapon in the East. His emphasis on psychological warfare is indicated in the following statement:

> It must be seen that where we find the psychological factors we should use them to our advantage and in this way save our resources and power. Doing so we can reach, with slight use of power, that which otherwise can be achieved only through hundreds of police battalions. . . .
>
> We must form there (in the East) a German rule which should be both stern and just. . . .
>
> If we follow these little things, we shall lead these peoples before they notice that their national independence is not anticipated within the frame of our permanent policy.[20]

Rosenberg's political schemes were not approved by the Fuehrer. Hitler worked out his own policy, and he outlined

[18] *Ibid*

[19] The totalitarian techniques of internal disintegration of their victims was applied by Rosenberg at the earlier stage of his Nazi career. Describing Rosenberg's activities as director of the Nazi Party's foreign office, the Canadian journalist, Robert Machray, caught the essence of Rosenberg's technique as early as 1934. He wrote "Rosenberg is doing everything he can to promote and assist revolution *from within* in those parts of Europe that are included in the general Nazi plan for Third Reich Officially, Berlin would deny having anything whatever to do with the revolution, which would be represented as a spontaneous "national" movement and, of course, welcomed with suitable action taken there anent. To some readers all this may suggest that Rosenberg is copying the strategy of Soviet Russia, at least in its earlier phase of Bolshevik aggressiveness, while others may consider that what has been said of his policy is so wildly fantastic as to be beyond belief (Robert Machray, "Hitler's Trail Over Europe," *The Fortnightly Review,* June, 1934).

[20] *Trial of War Criminals,* XXXIX, 414.

his political thinking on July 16, 1941, in a conference with
Rosenberg, Lammers, Keitel, and Goering. His pattern for an
appeal to the Eastern nations was:

> We shall always emphasize that we were compelled
> to occupy an area in order to make it safe and orderly;
> that we do it in the interest of the population, providing
> peace, food, traffic, etc. This (excuse) should be given as
> a reason for our regulations (measures). Our policy (or
> measures) should not indicate, however, that it prepares a
> way for the final settlement. All the necessary measures—
> executions, resettlement, etc.—we do in spite of it (in spite
> of our excuses) and we can do them in spite of it.[21]

The details followed:

> Crimea must be cleared of all foreigners and settled by
> Germans. In the same way the old-Austrian Galicia should
> become a Reichsgebet . . . . Volga Colony should come
> under German suzerainity, and Baku should become a
> German concession . . . . We must make a Garden of Eden
> of the newly acquired territories in the East.[22]

Full of ideas on how to bring about a German colonization
in the shortest possible time, Hitler rejected plans for the creation of semi-independent states or military formations in the
conquered areas of the East. Such a policy would be contrary
to his racial principles and antithetical to his planned extermination of the Slavs. His attitude toward cooperation with the
nations that fell under his sway during the German expansion
toward the East was stated by him in the following passage:

> Even if it appears to us easy to induce some of the
> conquered peoples to give military aid, the conception is
> false. It will turn inevitably against us one day. Only
> Germans may bear arms, not the Slavs, not the Czech,
> not the Cossack or Ukrainian.[23]

Hitler concluded his conference with a remark that his plans
for the East would remain unchangeable, and he was true to his
word. Although this line soon proved inexpedient and even
disastrous for the Germans, it prevailed in spite of many warnings, protests, and even contrary actions taken by Rosenberg's
Ostministerium and by some German army and SS circles.

[21] *Ibid.*, XXXVIII, p. 87, Doc. 221-L.
[22] *Ibid.*
[23] *Ibid.*

The Soviet Union Before and Shortly After the German Assault

When the German troops opened hostilities against the Soviet Union on June 22, 1941, they met an enemy whose arms and training they largely underestimated. According to German intelligence reports, the Soviet forces on the German eastern boundary amounted to 100 infantry divisions, 30 armored divisions, and 25 cavalry divisions.[24] Their total number roughly equalled the attacking German troops, but the Germans regarded the Soviet forces as inferior to them in fire power, mechanization, and training.[25] As the campaign proceeded, the Germans were surprised to learn that the Soviet troops had more self-propelled guns, war planes,[26] and tanks, and that the quality of the tanks was superior to those of the Germans. General Guderian[27] mentions that, at the time of assault, German armies possessed only 3,000 tanks against 17,000 Russian tanks. Hitler, when confronted with this evidence, declared to Guderian that he would have never started a war against the Soviet Union had he been informed about those odds.[28] To make matters worse, the Germans learned that their 37-millimeter anti-tank gun was ineffective against the Soviet T-34 tank, and that they had no armored weapon which could cope successfully with this steel Soviet monster.[29]

Besides considerable achievements in war production and military technology, the Soviet Union was by no means backward in her military training. Since 1930 there had been an increase of military training in the Soviet Union, which included not only the training of professionals and recruits for the Red army but a widespread teaching of military art in Soviet high schools, universities, and technical schools. These training schools produced 200,000 reserve officers in 1932, and 1,120,000 in 1935.[30] Also organized were specialized clubs within the

[24] *Trial of War Criminals Top Secret Conference of Hitler with O K W., Feb 3, 1941, concerning "Action Barbarossa,"* Doc 872-PS

[25] *Trial of War Criminals,* Doc 1017-PS

[26] War Department, *The World at War, 1939-1944* (Washington. The Infantry Journal, 1945), p 83

[27] General Heinz Guderian had been chief of panzer troops and chief of mobile troops in 1938, general-inspector of armored troops since February, 1943, and chief of general staff since July, 1944

[28] General Heinz Guderian, *Panzer Leader* (New York E. P Dutton & Co., 1952), p 190.

[29] *Ibid ,* p 248

[30] B. Mykhalchuk, "Introduction to the Study of the Red Army," *Development of State,* (Autumn, 1954).

Komsomol and different sports organizations for the promotion
of military knowledge. Examples of these clubs are the Voro-
shilov Sharp-shooters and Aeroclub. Soviet authorities secured
3,000 trained pilots in 1935 and 8,000 in 1936 from the training
of the Soviet Aeroclub. The number of paratroopers which the
Aeroclub produced was 4,500 in 1934, 16,000 in 1935, and 20,000
in 1936.[31]

How modernized and mechanized the Red army was in 1936
can be seen from the following article in the British newspaper
Daily Express, May 3, 1936:

> A sensational film of the Soviet Army maneuvers at
> Kiev last autumn was shown privately by the Russian Am-
> bassador at the Soviet Embassy last night.
>
> A series of scenes never before attempted at war—or
> on the screen—succeeded each other with breath-taking
> rapidity. . . .
>
> I have never seen such a striking shot as the surprise
> transportation by air of whole divisions behind the enemy
> lines. . . .
>
> Squadron after squadron of bombers followed, land-
> ing not only thousands of troops, but also lorries, artillery
> and tanks clutched to the fuselage between the landing
> wheels. Within a few minutes the whole division—Lewis
> gunners, mechanized troops, artillery and tanks—rushed
> into action, attacking the enemy in the rear.[32]

Although we do not possess statistics on the Soviet military
developments in the years 1936-1941, it can be assumed that the
Soviet military effort was increased during these years. Soviet
aid to Republican Spain during the Spanish Civil War, the real
possibility of Soviet intervention in Czechoslovakia in 1938,
clashes with Japan on the Manchurian border, and the imminent
danger of a Hitler invasion, urged the Soviet Union to increase
rather than decrease her military efforts. The military and
political steps which the Soviet Union took during the uneasy
peace with Germany, 1939-1941, show that the Soviet Union
was not taken by surprise by the German attack of 1941. The
book, *The World at War*, describes the Soviet political and
military preparatory steps as follows:

> While Hitler was busy conquering Poland, Western
> Europe, and the Balkans, the USSR prepared to resist

[31] *Ibid* , p. 248.
[32] Zelda and Coates, *op. cit.*, p. 557.

him. The Russians pushed their frontiers westward at
every opportunity to gain a buffer zone of defense against
invasion. East Poland was annexed to the geographic
frontier of the Bug river (September 17-29, 1939). Bessarabia and northern Bukovina were taken back from Rumania (June 27, 1940). The Baltic states of Estonia, Latvia,
and Lithuania were occupied and incorporated in the
Soviet Union (Aug. 29, 1940). A war against Finland
won defensive space for Leningrad and control of the
Gulf of Finland.[33]

Soviet preparation for war reached its final stages.
The quick triumph of Germany over the Balkan countries
pushed Russia into signing a neutrality pact with Japan
(April 13, 1941) to secure her Siberian frontier and
escape a war on two fronts. The best trained of all Russian generals, Gregor K. Zhukov, became Chief of Staff
in February, 1941; in May Stalin publicly centralized all
power in himself by taking the title of Premier. Russia
was warned in the previous winter by both Churchill
and Sumner Welles, then American Undersecretary of
State, that Hitler plotted attack.[34]

In view of the fact that the Soviet Union anticipated Hitler's
attack and that she had prepared for it for a long time, that she
had just one front on which to fight, that she had able generals,
that she had numerically superior manpower and arms, that her
military technique was one of the most modern in the world,
several questions must be asked. One must ask why Hitler
succeeded, in spite of all these facts, in reaching the gates of
Moscow within a few months, conquering almost all Ukraine,
taking 3,806,000 prisoners of war,[35] and bringing under his control a territory twice as large as France?

It would be a fallacy to explain Russian territorial losses in
terms of a tactical retreat, similar to the Russian retreat during
the Napoleonic invasion. The Red army, unlike the Russian
army in 1812, did not avoid battles but fought them almost on
their boundaries, lost them with the heaviest of casualties, and
only then retreated eastward. Another striking difference between the 1812 and 1941 campaigns is in the number of prisoners
of war. While the number of Russian prisoners of war taken in
1812, e.g., in the battle of Borodino, was the smallest that Napo-

---

[33] War Department, *The World at War*, p. 80
[34] *Ibid.*, p. 28.
[35] *Ibid*, p. 151.

leon experienced in all his battles throughout Europe,[36] the number of Red army war prisoners was the highest that Hitler had encountered in his career as conquerer of Europe. One would be puzzled forever by the mystery of early Soviet debacles and later Soviet victories if he were to fail to investigate two factors in the Soviet military potential—the fighting morale of the Red army on the one hand, and the sentiments of the Soviet population on the other.

The importance of the fighting morale of troops has been proved throughout all ages of human history. When we recall the classic example of 300 Spartans defending the passage of Thermopylae, or untrained French revolutionary troops resisting the Coalition, or the most recent examples where relatively insignificant Red Chinese forces defeated huge Chiang-Kai-Shek armies, we must agree that it is not only the physical but also the psychological factor which counts in war. A soldier must not only have something to fight with but also must have something to fight for.

What did the Red army have to fight for? Was it the regime, which through its policy of purges, arrests, resettlements, forceful collectivization, and elimination of hostile classes had injured almost every family in one or another way and had created a sense of political insecurity? B. Moore, Jr., using a statistical study of the experiences of Soviet refugees carried out by the Harvard project on the Soviet social system, describes this general feeling of political insecurity among the Soviet citizens very clearly:

> The burden of evidence now available indicates that the threat of arrest occurs as a very real possibility to a substantial portion of Soviet men, possibly as many as one in five at some point in their lives. . . . Out of a group of 1883 refugees who filled out questionnaires, about one-third (33 per cent) of the 1,290 men in this group reported that they themselves had undergone the experience of arrest. Slightly more than half (53 per cent) reported the arrest of a member of their immediate family.[37]

Or should they fight for the collective farms from which most of them came—farms which were not their own and which

---

[36] Ormand A L. Caulaincourt, *With Napoleon in Russia*, (New York. W Morrow and Co , 1935), pp. 102-103

[37] B. Moore, Jr , *Terror and Progress USSR*, (Cambridge. Harvard University Press, 1954), p 155

failed to prevent food shortages not only in big cities but also in the country? The economic circumstances in the big cities of the Soviet Union on the eve of war can be pictured by the following description of Odessa by Fred Virski, then a member of the Red army:

> On the Feldman Boulevard I found the Hotel Inturist, designed for foreigners and Russian big shots. One day it was my job to take some cases from the station to the Inturist. A waiter who spoke French showed me the menu. It was no more modest than a menu in the most elegant hotels in the 'rotten capitalistic world.' Two blocks away, leading to a store, I watched a mile-long line of men and women waiting with ration cards, of course, to buy potatoes and bread. The citizen of a country which at one time used to be the granary of Europe received four hundred grams of black, clayish, badly baked bread.[38]

Similar circumstances prevailing in the country are reported by Joseph Czapski at the outbreak of the war:

> On one occasion a peasant asked us why we wanted to fight. He himself had no intention of risking his life for the Soviets. If he took up arms at all, it would be against the 'red swine.' 'Formerly,' he said, 'we could stuff ourselves to here!'—raising his hand to the level of his beard; 'a cow cost 40 rubles, today it costs 3,000. There are 180 houses in our village. We have neither sugar nor bread.'[39]

The impact which the Soviet economic order and its political repercussions have had directly on the Soviet citizens and indirectly through them on the fighting morale of the Red army is reflected in reminiscences of the American diplomat in Moscow, Charles W. Thayer:

> Just before the Germans attacked the Russians I spent a night in a small Russian village about 100 miles west of Moscow. These villagers had been forcibly collectivized. Many had been exiled to Siberia. All had had their grain seized at confiscatory prices. Their resentment was so strong that an Internal Security Guard was stationed in the village. All night long an NKVD soldier

---

[38] Fred Virski, *My Life in the Red Army*, (New York: The Macmillan Co., 1949), p 41

[39] Joseph Czapski, *The Inhuman Land*, (New York Sheed & Ward, Inc, 1952), p 15

patrolled the muddy village street with a rifle on his shoulder.

Yet despite the soldier, the villagers had one by one sneaked through the back door of the hut where I was staying, to tell the foreigner their woes. 'Stalin can't fight Hitler because we won't' they told me. 'If they give us guns to fight, we'll know whom to use them against—and it won't be Hitler.'

I went back to Moscow deeply impressed. I had similar experiences in other Russian villages and I wrote a telegram to Washington with my conclusions: The Kremlin, I said, cannot risk a war with Germany because of the unreliability of the peasantry from which the army is largely recruited.[40]

To supplement the popular sentiments against the Soviet regime which prevailed in the Red army on the eve of the German attack, Fred Virski is quoted again:

Now, being ourselves in that army, we were naturally able to observe much more than before. It was certain that morale was very unsatisfactory. I did not meet anyone, except maybe Politruk[41] or his aide pompolit, who did not talk against the regime.[42]

One may ask if the ideology of Communism was not strong and worthwhile enough, especially for the young Soviet generation, to cause an eager defense of the Soviet regime? The answer was given in the negative by the Soviet government. With the outbreak of war, the Soviet government proclaimed it not as an ideological war of Communism against Fascism but as a Russian Fatherland war. This proves that the Communist ideology was not strong enough in the army or among the masses to be relied upon. The tradition of military glory was symbolized not by the heroes of the Russian Revolution or of International Communism but by such old Russian "bourgeois" and "reactionary" national heroes as Czar Ivan the Terrible, Peter the Great, General Kutusov, etc. By reviving Russian nationalism and pretending to be a savior of "Holy Russia," the Soviet government grasped one of the main assets of its survival, and it used this asset with a great skill in the time to come.

---

[40] Charles W Thayer, "Can Russia Trust Her 'Slave Armies'?" *The Saturday Evening Post*, (Aug. 7, 1954).

[41] Politruk—name for Political Commissar in Red Army, in charge of political education and indoctrination.

[42] Virski, *op. cit*, p. 71.

The revival and tenets of Russian nationalism were, however, of little use in securing the allegiance of the non-Russian Soviet Republics. Here, the German invasion was just a replacement of one foreign occupation by another. Within the Russian ethnographic territory there are some examples, even early in the war, of heroic participation by the populations of Moscow and Leningrad. Such accounts from the Baltic states, Byelo-, Russia, and Ukraine are lacking. To the contrary, withdrawal of the Red army from these areas was regarded as a signal for the creation of an independent national life which, however, was stopped abruptly by the German administration.[43]

[43] Kordt, *op. cit.*, pp. 309-310.

German Administrative Division, 1941-1944,
And the Ukrainian Ethnographic Boundary

Numbered areas on the map should be read as follows. 1 and 2—enlarged East Prussia, 3—Reichs-Commissariat Ukraine, 4—area under German military occupation; 5—district of Galicia, a part of General Gouvernement, 6—Carpatho-Ukraine, 7—Northern Bukovina; 8—Transnistria, area under Rumanian occupation; 9—Reichs-Commissariat Ostland.

CHAPTER 3

GERMAN OCCUPATION POLICY AT WORK

Justice in the life of a Nation is only the result of its power.[1]

Gentlemen. I am known as a brutal dog. Because of this reason I was appointed as a Reichskommissar of the Ukraine. Our task is to suck from the Ukraine all the goods we can get hold of,· without consideration of the feeling or the property of the Ukrainians.

Gentlemen: I am expecting from you the utmost severity towards the native population.[2]

Once we have won the war, then for all I care, mincemeat can be made of Poles and the Ukrainians and all the others who run around here.[3]

The Administrative Aspects of German Policy

THE BLUEPRINT for the German occupation of Ukraine was drawn by Hitler himself during a conference with the highest Nazi officials on July 16, 1941. He outlined the purpose of German occupation policy in the following statement:

Basically it is important that we dismember this big cake in a handy way so that we can: 1) occupy it, 2) administer it, 3) exploit it.[4]

At the same conference, Hitler expressed his hostility to the idea of cooperation with the nations of the Soviet Union, and repeated his intention to keep them suppressed by physical force and harsh administrative measures. Therefore, Ukraine was to be included in the general pattern of German policy regarding Eastern Europe, and Rosenberg's idea of a National

---

[1] Joseph Goebbels, *Was auf dem Spiele Steht*, Sept 27, 1942, from *Der Steile Aufstieg* (speeches and articles, 1942-43)

[2] Erich Koch's Inauguration Speech, Rovno, Sept , 1941, in J Thorwald, *Wen Sie Verderben Wollen*, (Stuttgart. Steingrueben Verlag, 1951), p. 74

[3] Speech of Governor General Hans Frank, Jan. 14, 1944, in Lukacs, *op cit.*, p 570.

[4] *Trial of War Criminals, op. cit* , Doc 221-L.

Ukrainian state as an conterpoise against Russia was dropped. Ukrainian nationalism was regarded by Hitler as a potential enemy of Germany and of his plans of colonization. Ukraine was to be divided into three parts. Bessarabia, Northern Bukovina, and a portion of Southern Ukraine between the Dnister and Boh Rivers (Transnistria) were to be put under the temporary administration of Rumania. Western Ukraine, which belonged to Austria before World War I, was to be included within the Polish territory under German occupation (General Government). The rest of Ukraine was to be included in the Reichskommissariat Ukraine.

The real administration of the Reichskommissariat Ukraine extended over the central Ukrainian provinces, and Volynia Podolia, and a part of Polissya; the eastern part of Ukraine (Donbas area and Kharkiv) remained under German military administration until the end of the occupation. The Reichs-kommissariat Ukraine was ruled by the iron hand of Reichs-kommissar Erich Koch who was, to a great degree, the actual implementer of Hitler's plans in Eastern Europe. All key administration in the Reichskommissariat was in German hands. The General Kommissars administered the larger subregions called General-Bezirke, and the Gebiets Kommissars ruled over the smaller administrative units, named Kreisgebiets.[5] Stadt-kommissars and Landwirtschaftsfuehrer supervised the administration of rayons,[6] municipalities, and villages, and all of them were actually subordinated to Koch. The formal superior position of the *Ostministerium,* under the leadership of Rosenberg, was a fiction, because Erich Koch managed to establish close direct contact with Hitler and could afford to go over the head of Rosenberg.[7] Virtually supreme, Reichskommissar Koch was, nevertheless, somewhat limited in his authority. The German police in this area were subordinate to Himmler, chief of the German Gestapo. Economic planning and exploitation of the natural resources of the Reichskommissariat were set up under Reichsmarshal Goering, who acted as head of the German

[5] There were six Generalbezirke in the Reichskommissariat Ukraine by September, 1942. Volynia-Podolia, Zhytomyr, Kiev, Dnipropetrovsk, Nykolayev, and Crimea. The Generalbezirke were subdivided into 114 Kreisgebiete

[6] Rayon was the smallest administrative unit which consisted of a group of villages and was administered by Ukrainian Rayonchefs (See: *Voelkisher Beobachter,* April 11, 1942). There were 443 rayons in the Reichs-kommissariat Ukraine.

[7] Kleist, *Zwischen Hitler und Stalin,* p. 181.

Four-Year Plan. The railways and mail were under military authorities. In order to overcome differences in policy arising from the conflicting authorities, the Reichskommissar had special liaison officers in his headquarters. With the help of these officers, he coordinated the work with the agencies which were not under his control.[8]

Similar administrative arrangements prevailed in Western Ukraine which was put under the administration of the General-government as the District of Galizien. The Governor General, Hans Frank, exercised the same authority as the Reichskommissar and had the same limitations regarding the Gestapo, Economic Commissions, and Railways and Mail Agency. Instead of different Kommissars in the General Government there were governors administering districts and Kreishauptmanns administering the Kreise. The cities were supervised by Stadthauptmanns. All of them were subordinated to Governor General Frank.

There was a difference in the legal standing between the Reichskommissar and Governor General. This was true because while the first was formally subordinated to Ostminister Rosenberg, the latter enjoyed the rank of a Reichsminister himself and was formally subordinate only to Hitler.

There was also some difference in the degree of self-government of the non-German population in the two occupation areas. In the Reichskommissariat Ukraine, the native population was allowed to form only local municipal and village governments. In the General Government, the non-German population was represented in the local governments mentioned and also was allowed to form Jewish, Polish, and Ukrainian Aid Committees. Such aid committees were centralized civil agencies, with branches scattered throughout the General Government. They acted as links between the respective nationalities and the German authorities. With the help of the "Aid Committees," the Western Ukrainians were able to get minor concessions from the Germans, such as opening high schools, starting summer camps for youth, and conducting welfare activities in hospitals and orphanages. The Germans tried to use these committees to get statistical data in order to influence the population to give speedy delivery of the prescribed goods and to encourage young people to enlist for work in Germany. This "privilege"

[8] *Trial of War Criminals, op. cit.,* Doc. 1058. See also *Encyclopedia of Ukraine,* I, 584.

of having an "Aid Committee" was actually politically insignificant. It by no means indicated the abandonment of German annihilation and colonization policies in this region. The best proof of this is that all of the Jews in General Government were annihilated in spite of a Jewish "Aid Committee."[9]

Policy of Annihilation

In anticipation of a large-scale colonization in Ukraine, the Germans were faced with the problem of determining what should happen to the masses of the native population in this area. Ukraine, with a population density of 66 persons per square kilometer (only 10% lower than that of France),[10] was ill adapted for colonization. Acting in the spirit of Nazi ideology, which claimed all rights for the "master race" and provided none such for the "races" branded as "inferior" or "harmful," the Germans considered several drastic measures and started actions designed to create the *Lebensraum*. The plans may be put in three main categories: 1) biological reduction; 2) dispersion of the native population as slave labor throughout the whole German empire, and 3) large-scale resettlement of the native population in an eastward direction.

One of the earliest measures which the Germans applied in Ukraine was that of biological reduction. The first victims of the German annihilation policy were the Jews who numbered three millions at the time of the German conquest.[11] They were to be destroyed completely as a "harmful and conspiring nation," although it is difficult to understand in what way the scattered Ukrainian Jewish minority could challenge the mighty conqueror since they had lost their main assets, capital, and freedom of enterprise under the Soviets. The Jews were brought from the villages and small towns and were concentrated in county and district cities, where they were put in segregated ghettos. Many of them died from disease and undernourishment, but the bulk of the Jewish population was annihilated through mass executions which started as early as the autumn of 1941. By the end of 1941, the number of Ukrainian Jews executed reached 200,000, according to official German documents. During the following year, the Jewish population was divided into classes according to the needs of the German army and administration.

[9] *Encyclopedia of Ukraine*, p. 176.
[10] *Encyclopedia of Ukraine*, p. 168.
[11] *Ibid*, "Nationality Status," p. 176.

The mass executions proceeded so that the least productive classes were destroyed first, followed by the other classes. The "action" against the Jews was completed by the spring of 1943, when the Jews officially ceased to exist in the Reichskommissariat of Ukraine and in the General Government. The only discoverable reason for the liquidation of the Jews was the German racial ideology. From the standpoint of military expediency or economic advantage, these mass executions were a grave mistake. The Jewish population of Ukraine constituted the largest reservoir of skilled artisans and professional people who, having lived in the turbulent circumstances of Eastern Europe for centuries, were used to shifting their loyalties to any established authority. That there were no sporadic anti-German actions on the part of the Jewish minority can be seen from the following report of an officer of the German Economic Commission in Ukraine dated Dec. 2, 1941:

> The attitude of the Jewish population was from the beginning rather shy and willing. They tried to avoid any conflicts with the German Administration. . . . It cannot be proved that the Jews participated in an organized manner in any sabotage action against the Germans. It cannot be asserted that the Jews represented a danger to the German Army. With the work performed by the Jews, which, of course, was stimulated by fear, the German Army and Administration was completely satisfied.[12]

A hint of economic difficulties which the sudden liquidation of the Jews in Ukraine brought about is seen in the following comment in Reichskommissar Koch's report to the Fuehrer:

> I have lost 500,000 Jews. I had to eliminate them because the Jews are a harmful element. But in this territory they were the only artisans. . . . I have not a sufficient number of shoemakers to repair shoes for our employees. I can not get them; there are no artisans since the Jews were liquidated.[13]

In regard to Ukraine and the other nations in the prospective German settlement areas, the main objective of German policy was not annihilation of the total population but a considerable reduction of their numbers. The Germans sought to eliminate

[12] *Trials of War Criminals, op. cit ,* XXXII, 72-75
[13] Fuehrer's conference with Field Marshall Keitel and Gen. Zeitzler on Berghof, June 8, 1943, quoted from the journal, *Development of State,* Cleveland, (Summer, 1954), No 2 (13) sec. *Documents.*

the more demonstrative elements and to reduce the rest to a passive mass which had a deeply impressed inferiority complex, without higher goals and ambitions. The Germans could then handle them at will. One of the most successful measures to reduce numbers which the Germans applied in Ukraine was artificial famine. The famine was due partially to the war damage and partially to flooding of crop lands in the summer of 1941. But these damages were local, and there were many untouched areas with plenty of surplus food. However, the German authorities forbade the transportation of food to needy regions, and the guards posted on the highways and at railway stations confiscated all food that persons might be carrying. Thus, many village regions which were deprived of their grain stocks by flood or war were isolated and condemned to starvation as were the areas of the Carpathian Mountains and the northern swampy parts of Ukraine which were not self sufficient.[14]

The cities of Ukraine were assigned to starvation rations which omitted milk, fat, and sometimes even bread. All ways of getting additional food were legally forbidden. The free food markets were confiscated, and the transportation of food to cities was checked.[15] Other places where the starvation policy was applied with great success were the camps in which Soviet prisoners of war were held. Here the Germans had a chance to eliminate the youngest, healthiest, and potentially most reproductive portion of a nation. In the winter of 1941-1942, hundreds of thousands of Soviet prisoners of war were deliberately let starve or else died from plagues.[16] The starvation policy is clearly reflected also in the documents of the time. Count Ciano, Italian foreign minister, recalls in his *Diary* that in his talk with Reichsmarshal Goering in November, 1941, Goering pointed to the starvation of Russian prisoners of war as an example of ways to bring about the decimation of a nation.[17] Similar indications of German famine policy are reflected in the report by an Economic Commission officer from Ukraine dated Dec. 2, 1941:

> If we shoot the Jews, liquidate the war prisoners, starve the major part of the big cities' population, and in

[14] Author's personal experience
[15] *Encyclopedia of Ukraine*, p. 583, (see also *Trial of War Criminals*, Doc. 303-PS).
[16] *Trial of War Criminals, op. cit.,* XXIX, 112.
[17] Lukacs, *op. cit*, p 458.

the coming year reduce also a part of the peasants through famine there will rise a question: Who is going to produce the economic goods?[18]

The extent of this famine is apparent from a passage in Goebbels' *Diary*[19] from March, 1942:

The food situation in the occupied eastern areas is exceptionally precarious. Thousands and tens of thousands are dying of hunger without anybody even raising a finger.[20]

Besides the reduction of population by starvation, the Germans used other means such as shooting hostages in a proportion of 50 to 100 for each German killed,[21] using Soviet prisoners for especially hazardous tasks such as clearing out land mines,[22] and instructing their police in eastern areas not to prevent plagues and to promote immorality.[23] Promotion of drinking among the population was also one of the means of biological destruction. The German authorities arranged that peasants who delivered food were to be partially paid in whisky which became popular under the name of *kontygentivka*.[24] Enlightening in this respect are the remarks which Hitler made during one of his table talks at his headquarters in Vinnitsia (Ukraine) in the summer of 1942. Stimulated and aroused by the report of Martin Bormann, who had just returned from a tour through the Ukrainian kolkhoses and who told him about the general healthy appearance of the Ukrainians and the abundance of children, Hitler spent a considerable time reflecting on German policy toward the non-German population in the East. In this talk, he turned violently against the prohibition of abortions in the East and urged an increasing supply of mechanical means of contraception in these areas to lower the birth rate of the "race" destined for a gradual annihilation. In his eagerness and excitement, Hitler even threatened to shoot any German official

[18] *Trial of War Criminals, op cit*, XXII, 72-75.
[19] Joseph Goebbels, Nazi Minister of Propaganda
[20] Louis D Lochner, *The Goebbels Diaries*, (Garden City, N Y Doubleday and Co , Inc , 1948), p 115.
[21] *Trial of War Criminals*, Doc. 389-PS, *Keitel's Top-Secret Directive*
[22] *Ibid*, XXVII, p. 68, *Top-Secret Draft*, Nov. 11, 1941, of a memorandum on Goering's statement at a conference on Nov 7, 1941
[23] I. Krypyakevich, *History of the Ukrainian Armed Forces*, (Winnipeg: Ukrainian Book Club, 1953), p. 656.
[24] Author's own experience. *Kontygentivka* derives its name from *kontingent* —the German designation of compulsory farm deliveries under the German occupation.

in the East who acted contrary to this policy.[25] Sanitary measures and medical care also were shaped to serve the Nazi
Lebensraum policy in the East and not the welfare of its inhabitants. This can be perceived from the following words of Hitler:

> If we should try to establish a health service accord-
> ing to German standards for the non-German population
> in the Occupied East, it would be a madness. The vacci-
> nation and the other preventive health measures could
> not apply to the non-German population. We should,
> therefore, unperturbedly spread the superstitions among
> them arguing that vaccination is very harmful to health.[26]

These remarks by Hitler indicate clearly that police and
administrative measures in Ukraine regarding sanitation and
medical facilities were not accidental nor were they due solely
to abuses by local German authorities or to the personal brutality of Reichskommissar Koch or Governor General Frank. Such
measures were parts of a premeditated and consistent pattern
of the *Lebensraum* policy.

German Policy of Enslavement

The enslavement policy contained many aspects which were
intended to reduce the nations in annexed territories to a subhuman status. One of these measures was to deprive the population of their leading and better educated classes and to prevent the masses from securing an education by closing schools
and museums, and by destroying memorials and centers of
culture which would remind the masses of something better
and more worthwhile than the basic needs of life.

The leading class of Poland, which was one of the first
Eastern European countries designated as a settlement area,
was the initial group of its kind to feel the force of German
policy. As early as 1940, Bormann, who was later second to
Hitler in the National-Socialist Party, said:

> The Fuehrer had to emphasize once more that for
> Poles there can be just one ruler—the German. There
> could not be two Lords side by side; therefore all repre-
> sentatives of the Polish intelligentsia are to be liquidated.
> It sounds hard but it is the law of life. . . . The General

---

[25] *Trial of War Criminals*, Doc. 172-USSR.
[26] Henry Picker, *Hitler Tischgespraeche, im Fuehrerhauptquartier, 1941-42,*
    Hitler's table talk on evening of July 22, 1942, (Bonn. Athenaeum-
    Verlag, 1951), p. 116.

Government is a Polish reservation—a big Polish labor camp.[27]

A year later when Western Ukraine was incorporated into the General Government, Governor General Hans Frank endorsed a similar policy toward the Ukrainians:

First of all we should not let the Ukrainians of our District of Galizien believe that we were ready to recognize any independent Ukrainian State within the territories destined for the Great German Reich. . . . I see a solution of the Ukrainian problem in this way, that they should, similar to the Poles, remain at our disposal as a working power in the future [28]

Thus, the level of the population which the Germans intended to preserve in the East was not supposed to rise above that of a working animal. Every one above this level was to be eliminated. Enlightening is an incident which occurred during Rosenberg's visit to Ukraine in the summer of 1943. Rosenberg still defended a more conciliatory treatment of the Ukrainians, especially during the war, and he suggested to Koch that he invite a few outstanding Ukrainians to dine with them. Koch's reply to this proposal was very characteristic:

If I should find a Ukrainian who is worthy to sit with me at the table I must let him be shot. . . .[29]

Koch turned against the intellectual and cultural activities in Ukraine, regarding them as an inspiration against German policy. In his report on March 16, 1943, he tried to point out to Rosenberg that the Ukrainian intellectuals and the former emigrants were the moving forces of the Ukrainian national independence movement which was irreconcilable with German objectives in Ukraine.

Also *Proswita*[30] where it still exists serves as a disguised institution for Ukrainian chauvinists. Ukrainian teachers from *Proswita* participated in the activities of the Ukrainian Resistance Army in Kamin-Koshyrsk.[31]
The Ukrainian emigrants succeeded in spreading their

---

[27] *Ibid*
[28] *Trial of War Criminals,* XXIX, 50
[29] Thorwald, J , *Wen Sie Verberden Wollen,* (Stuttgart: Steingrueben Verlag, 1952), p 239
[30] Traditional Ukrainian Cultural and Educational Community Center.
[31] *Trial of War Criminals,* Doc 192-PS

influence on Bandera and Melnyk movements[32] both of which are consciously anti-German.[33]

The destruction of Ukrainian intelligentsia started as early as the winter of 1941-42. There were arrests and executions in the principal cities of Ukraine, such as Kiev, Kharkiv, Dnipropetrovsk, Nykolayev, Kamenets-Podilskyi, and others.[34] When the partisan warfare began, the Germans made it their policy to take their hostages first of all from the intelligentsia. Still more was done by the Germans to prevent the creation of a new intelligentsia, and this was regarded as so important that the Fuehrer stressed it in his order determining the German policy in Eastern Europe.[35] Hitler also was concerned with this issue in his table talks and one of them, which is quoted here, is interesting because it reveals his fears and the reasons which had caused him to order the above mentioned measure.

> It is especially important to avoid any measures which would awake among the non-German population a feeling for self-government. . . . For this reason we cannot give to the non-German population any chances for higher education. If we would commit such a mistake we would plant the roots of resistance against our rule by ourselves. We would have to give them the schools, in which they would have to pay for attendance. But they should not be taught more than the reading of the traffic signs. . . . Beyond this it would be sufficient if the non-German population acquires some reading and writing knowledge of German. An education in counting and the similar disciplines is superfluous. . . .[36]

Koch was so eager to follow these directives that he was even reluctant to open the elementary schools in Ukraine. As to the extent of education in Ukraine, there seemed to be sharp disagreement between the Reichskommissariat and the *Ostministerium*. The feud went so far that a deputy of Koch, named Dargel, appeared personally in the Department of Education in *Ostministerium* and caused a wild scene by an attack on the

[32] Both movements were the offsprings of the Ukrainian Nationalist Organization. (OUN)
[33] *Trial of War Criminals*, Doc 192-PS.
[34] *Encyclopedia of Ukraine*, p 585.
[35] *Trial of War Criminals*, Doc. 045-PS.
[36] Picker, *op. cit.*, p 116.

chief of the department, Mr. Milwe. The dialogue which ensued on this particular occasion is too characteristic to be omitted:

Dargel: . . . do you wish to create an Ukrainian educated class at the time when we want to annihilate the Ukrainians?

Milwe: You are not able to annihilate 40 millions.

Dargel: It is our business.

Milwe: And what shall become of Ukraine?

Dargel: Are you really living on the moon? You should know that, according to the will of the Fuehrer, the Ukraine should become a space for settlement of German peasants.[37]

This anti-intellectual policy also embraced attacks on the cultural centers and historical monuments in Ukraine. Significant is an extract from the order to the German troops, signed by Fieldmarshal Reichenau, dated Oct. 10, 1941:

The Soviets, during their retreat, have often set the houses on fire. Our troops are to extinguish the fires only when it is necessary for the securing of Army quarters. Otherwise the disappearance of the symbols of the former Bolshevist rule, also in forms of buildings, are included in our fight of annihilation. Therefore, neither historical nor Fine Arts objects deserve any consideration here in the East.[38]

Following this attitude, the Nazi plundered, destroyed or transported libraries, museums, and scientific institutions to Germany. Among others, they barbarously destroyed the Library of the Ukrainian Academy of Sciences in Kiev, transported the whole Kiev city library to Germany and partially plundered the university library in Kharkiv.[39] A political report from Kiev by Paul W. Thompson, German professor of Posen University, dated in the autumn of 1942, comments on this policy as follows:

Our behavior toward cultural and economic institutions caused bitter disappointment in the circles of the intelligentsia.[40]

This anti-cultural campaign in Ukraine seemed to have two main objectives: a) To deprive the enslaved Ukrainian masses

[37] Thorwald, *op cit*, pp. 179-182
[38] *Trial of War Criminals*, I, 84
[39] *Encyclopedia of Ukraine*, I, 1015
[40] *Trial of War Criminals*, Doc 303-PS.

of the objects of their tradition and of any thoughts loftier than the manual work for which they were destined; b) to eliminate the symbols of non-Germanic cultural achievements in the areas destined for Teutonic colonization.

Besides steps for the spiritual sterilization of the Slavic masses in Eastern Europe, actions were taken to bring about physical enslavement. The campaign in Eastern Europe prolonged, the Germans felt a need to replenish their troops with new reserves, and many workers from their vital industries had to be drafted. To fill their places, the Germans were forced to import millions of foreign workers into Germany. The methods of enlistment and the working and living conditions which German authorities provided for workers from Eastern Europe were harsh and discriminatory. In Germany, the laborers from Ukraine and Poland were placed in barracks behind barbed wire, which were marked with discriminatory signs "Ost" or "Poland." Freedom of movement was restricted, and use of streetcars and of the cultural and recreational facilities was out of bounds. In general, the laborers were supposed to be treated in the same way as the Soviet prisoners of war, and Reichsmarshal Goering recommended that this category of foreign laborers be fed with cat and horsemeat.[41] For smaller transgressions, physical force was abundantly used to punish laborers; and for more grave transgressions, they were sent to the concentration camps from where there was no return. Adam Schmidt, a German railway worker from Essen and a witness before the Nuremberg Military Tribunal, described the treatment of workers from Eastern Europe:

> In the middle of 1941, there came the first workers from Poland, Galicien, and from Polish Ukraine. They arrived in freight trains which were built for transportation of potatoes, construction materials, and cattle, and they were employed in Krupp Industries.
>
> It was shocking for every honest German to see how these people were pushed, trampled upon, and generally treated. I could see with my own eyes how the sick, who could hardly walk, were brought to work.
>
> The same treatment was applied to the "Ost" workers, who came to Essen in the middle of 1942.[42]

[41] *Ibid*, XXVII, 67.
[42] *Ibid*, XXXV, 73-75.

Rumors about the treatment of workers from the East soon spread throughout Eastern Europe, and voluntary enlistment or even enlistment by assignment for work in Germany slowed or ceased. Then the German authorities applied most drastic measures of terror or force to secure a sufficient labor force. Villages which did not fulfill the assigned quota of laborers were visited by punitive expeditions. The houses of refugees were burned, or their relatives were kept in concentration camps until they appeared before enlisting commissions.[43] In addition, a large scale man hunt was arranged during which the people were caught without discrimination, and were loaded in the sealed freight trains and brought to Germany. In other cases, the captives were divided. The younger and stronger looking people were taken, and the others were left free. There were heart-breaking scenes when families were torn apart and children were taken from their mothers.[44] The workers were captured in public places such as on the streets, in railway stations, markets, and even in churches.[45] The former German consul in the Soviet Union and a member of the Political Department in the *Ostministerium* comments on this policy in his political report for Oct. 25, 1942:

> In the usual limitless mistreatment of Slavic peoples there were applied the "enlistment methods" which recall the darkest pages of the slave trade. There started a regular man hunt, and without regard to health, condition, or age, the people were deported to Germany.[46]

In this enslavement policy, Ukraine seemed to be of special interest to the Fuehrer. He was not satisfied with more Ukrainian slave labor but tried to transform a considerable part of the Ukrainian youth into Germans. Hitler's personal order of Oct. 9, 1942, required immediate deportation to Germany of 400,000 to 500,000 picked Ukrainian girls between the ages of 15 and 35. They were to be helpers in German households to further their Germanization and to help make them permanent residents of Germany. This mixing with an "inferior race" was a deviation from the strict racial laws which Hitler justified with historical reasons. He explained that a Gothic state existed many cen-

[43] *Ibid.*, XXV, 268.
[44] People from 14 years of age and up were eligible for forced labor in Germany (see *Encyclopedia of Ukraine*, p. 951).
[45] Thorwald, *op. cit.*, p. 86
[46] *Trial of War Criminals*, XXV, 331

turies ago in Ukraine and that his order merely meant the picking up of scattered "Germanic blood."[47]

Policy of Colonization

Although the war in the East was by no means concluded and although the Germans suffered some setbacks and heavy losses, the preparation for speedy colonization of Eastern Europe was by no means postponed. Five months after the incorporation of Western Ukraine into the General Government, Governor General Frank disclosed to his associates the coming colonization plans:

> . . . now it became quite clear that this area of General Government is bound to be included in the process of advancing German nationality toward the East, and already within a measurable space of time, in the settlement program of our people. . . .
>
> Being then in a position to push the foreign nationalities forward, we shall have no unsurmountable obstacles in establishing Germans here at the expense of the foreign element.
>
> Farther in the East there will be erected a Gothen province, and here in the General Government, we shall have a Vandalen province.[48]

Frank's words were not just theories because in 1942 the first large-scale German settlement was established in the Polish part of the General Government, in the vicinity of the town of Zamosc. In 1943, all measures were taken to start a mass resettlement in the Districts of Galizien and Lublin In the spring of the same year, German authorities sent some surveyors to measure the land in those areas. The Nuremberg Trial documents record a protest against such action by the head of the Ukrainian Aid Committee, Prof. Volodymyr Kubiyovych, who learned or rightly assumed the purpose of the survey.[49] The great resettlement actions affecting the Districts of Galizien and Lublin were timed for the late summer of 1943, but could not take place because of the invasion of the Kovpak Partisan Detachment in July of that year. Frank, faced with unexpected delay, agreed in a conference with the SS General Bach-Zelewsky that the planned resettlement should follow immediately after the liqui-

[47] *Ibid*, XXV, 83
[48] *Ibid*, XXIX, 501. Speech of Governor General Frank in Cracow, Dec. 16, 1941.
[49] *Ibid.*, Doc. 1526-PS.

dation of the "band."[50] But this action was destined never to occur. Although Kovpak's Red partisans withdrew from Western Ukraine in the beginning of the autumn of 1943, their appearance was followed by large scale National Ukrainian partisan warfare in this region. Frank was compelled to shelve the resettlement plans until the end of the war.

How strong the program of German colonization of Eastern Europe was rooted in the minds of leading Nazi officials is apparent in the speech of Himmler at an SS group leaders' meeting in Posen, Oct. 14, 1943. At this time, when the Germans had already lost half of Ukraine and when the German Eastern front was moving westward, Himmler still cherished a hope for large-scale German settlements in Eastern Europe. He said:

> We must establish in 20 to 30 years a ruling class throughout Europe. When we SS and the peasants together with our friend Backe[51] push forward a settlement there in the East, generously and without any restrictions regardless of the customs and with a dash and revolutionary impetus (Drang), then we shall push our boundary 500 kilometers eastwards in 20 years.[52]

In view of the German colonization plans, one can understand more easily the Nazi land policy in Ukraine. The Germans intended to preserve the Soviet collective system as much as possible because a transfer of the community lands or of state-owned lands seemed easier to them than the transfer of many individual farms. The control and exploitation of agricultural goods also seemed to be simpler in a collective farm system. Thus, Reichsminister Backe said at the outbreak of the Soviet-German war:

> If the kolchoses were not introduced by the Soviet authorities they were to be invented by the Germans.[53]

Therefore, Rosenberg's land edict of Feb. 15, 1942, left the collective farm system intact and only changed the name kolchose to Cooperative Farm and put it under local German control. The surplus produce of the Cooperative Farms was to be sold at nominal prices to the German authorities, and private

[50] *Ibid*, XXIX, 606.
[51] Herbert Backe, Nazi Minister of Food Supply.
[52] *Ibid*, XXIX, 171.
[53] Thorwald, *op cit*, p. 25.

trade was forbidden. Only in exceptional cases did the edict provide for individual cultivation of the soil (see section D-1 and E-1 of the edict).[54] These exceptional clauses had very limited application, and throughout all of the German occupation only 10 per cent of all land in Ukraine was under private cultivation.[55] Another and more liberal land edict was issued by Rosenberg on June 3, 1943. It provided for a distribution of land among all the peasants in the Eastern occupied areas who were able to cultivate it. The edict also promised land grants to all former soldiers of the Red army after the end of the war.[56] This clever move by Rosenberg, which came amidst German setbacks on the Eastern front and growing partisan warfare, was too late to change the basic attitude of the people. And the edict was proclaimed only in "Ostland." Erich Koch objected to the announcement of the edict in Ukraine and refused to put it into effect. Koch was supported wholeheartedly by Hitler. Thus, the colonial policy, in its unchanged form, remained as the only objective of the German authorities in Ukraine up to the very end of the occupation.

[54] Kleist, *Zwischen Hitler und Stalin*, see Appendix.
[55] *Trial of War Criminals*, Doc 294-PS
[56] Kleist, *Zwischen Hitler und Stalin*, p 317

CHAPTER 4

BETWEEN ANVIL AND HAMMER

The greatest reservoirs of anti-Bolshevik manpower—those in eastern Poland, the Baltics and in Ukraine—were left untouched, as the population of these territories was to be reduced to colonial status within the German eastern empire; on the other hand, loud huzzahs and spectacular celebrations greeted appearing Spanish Blue Divisions, "Wallon" and "French" SS-Legions . . .[1]

Otherwise there existed the possibility that Hitler would combine his anti-Bolshevik slogan with a call on nationalities to make themselves free, in order to weaken first of all the Great Russian nationalism. To equal surprise of friend and enemy of the Nazi state, Hitler chose no such approach, but retained foolish phantasies from his book *Mein Kampf.* . . . In the place of the crushed Soviet Union there should be created a "German India."[2]

I know by now what those Germans are like. I was looking for an idea . . . but they have none. They have organization, technique, and order. . . .[3]

A Chance Never to be Repeated

As THE WAR against the Soviet Union proceeded, it became clearer with the passing of each day that German military might alone was insufficient. The reserves of manpower and the quality of arms were inadequate to cope with the Red army and to hold the huge Eastern front. Some of the dangers of the Eastern campaign were anticipated by German Eastern European experts and military planners before the outbreak of hostilities, and most of the dangers were revealed during the

---

[1] Lukacs, *op cit.*, p. 415.

[2] Erich Kordt, *op cit*, p 310

[3] Gen Vlassov's words quoted from J Thorwald, *op. cit.*, p 282 Gen. A. Vlassov, one of the outstanding Soviet military leaders, was famous for his defense of Moscow in the autumn of 1941. Taken a prisoner of war by Germans in the spring of 1942, he expressed his willingness to co-operate with the Germans on the condition that a National Russian state be created after the defeat of the Soviet Union

campaign.[4] German troops were able to achieve some spectacular military victories in the early stage of the war. They took millions of prisoners of war and pushed hundreds of miles eastward. This was due, in great degree, to the unwillingness of the Red army to defend the Soviet government. The German view concerning the will of the Red army to resist German invasion is revealed in the following passage by Dr. Kleist:

> The German soldier soon noticed that the Red Army was composed of very different troop detachments. Only a few small special detachments fought stubbornly. The great majority of the Red soldiers was not influenced at all by a spirit of resistance. Whole divisions of the Red army disintegrated without a fight.[5]

The people of Soviet Ukraine were even more definitely not on the side of the Soviet regime. This can be perceived from the following lines in *The Goebbels Diaries*:

> The inhabitants of Ukraine were more than inclined at the beginning to regard the Fuehrer as the savior of Europe and to welcome the German Wehrmacht most cordially.[6]

Even in Russia proper, especially in the rural areas, the Germans were greeted as liberators. General Guderian, describing his military operations in the area of Smolensk and Moscow, recalls:

> A significant indication of the attitude of the civilian population is provided by the fact that women came out from their villages to the very battlefield bringing wooden platters of bread and butter and eggs and, in my case at least, refused to let me move on before I had eaten.[7]

There are some indications that the Russians were divided in their loyalty to the Soviet regime. It cannot be denied that the Soviet Union, in spite of her multi-national composition, was really dominated by Russians and that the German attack against the Soviet Union was in reality an attack against the Russian Empire. The Soviet Russian regime, combining in an amazing way the slogan of national self-determination and ruth-

---

[4] Guderian, *op. cit.*, pp 248 and 276.
[5] Kleist, *Zwischen Hitler und Stalin*, p 130.
[6] *The Goebbels Diaries*, trans by Louis P Lochner, (Fireside Press, Inc., 1948), p. 185.
[7] Guderian, *op. cit.*, pp. 193-194.

less force, was able to bring back into the Russian state many non-Russian nations separated from it during the Revolution of 1917. It was doubtful if a new Russia, emerging after defeat of the Soviet Russian regime, would be able to dominate these nations which were striving for independence. Many Russians defended the Soviet regime as a last possibility of maintaining the integrity of the Russian Empire. Others like General Vlassov believed that the Germans would help them rebuild the Soviet Russian empire into a National Russian empire. It is evident from questioning Soviet prisoners of war that many Russians considered the emancipation of the non-Russian nations as quite natural, and they were more eager to get rid of the Soviet regime than to preserve the Russian empire at the expense of their own human dignity.[8] Thus, it is to be assumed that if the Germans had instituted a just order in Eastern Europe, such as one based on Wilson's "14 points," they could have counted on considerable support even from the Great Russians. It is also apparent that such a program would have given the Germans the wholehearted support of the non-Russian nations that made up roughly half of the Soviet population. Neither the Baltic nations nor the Ukrainians nor the other non-Russian nations could maintain a loyal attachment to the Soviet Union. This would mean a Russian dictatorship as well as an inhuman social system. In the non-Russian areas occupied by the Germans, there sprung up genuine national movements which were both anti-Soviet and anti-Russian. In Lithuania, the Front of Lithuanian Activities (LAF), an underground organization, formed a provisional government on the second day of the German-Soviet war.[9] In Ukraine, a provisional National government was formed, and the independence of the Ukraine was proclaimed in Lviv (Western Ukraine) on June 30, 1941.[10] Similar in character were the Ukrainian National councils formed in Rovno (Volynia) in the middle of July, 1941, and in Kiev in October, 1941.[11] The Ukrainian National Partisan group, commanded by Otaman Bulba-Borowets, conducted operations against Soviet troops in the province of Polissya and coordinated its actions with those of the German army.[12] Throughout

---

[8] *Trial of War Criminals*, Doc 294-PS
[9] Krypyakevych, *op cit*, p. 653.
[10] Kleist, *Zwischen Hitler und Stalin*, p. 186.
[11] *Encyclopedia of Ukraine*, *op. cit.*, p. 584.
[12] *Ibid*, p 586.

Ukraine, the people who were liberated from the Red regime
started to organize their own administration, national press,
economic associations, cultural institutions, and schools. Former
Red army soldiers who either escaped the war or were freed
from stalags by the Germans went to work collecting the harvest
or rebuilding destroyed industrial plants.[13] There was strong
popular support in the Ukraine for organization of a National
Ukrainian army to fight the Red army and Bolshevism. The
time was ripe for the Germans to join forces with the national
movements within the Soviet Union and to utilize these forces
to bring about the complete annihilation of the Soviet regime.

But the Germans failed to use the forces which played into
their hands. Hitler pushed his brand of politics in Eastern
Europe, and his policies excluded cooperation with any national group in Eastern Europe. The German objective was
to secure the victory and to dominate Eastern Europe by military and police force.

Because of the uncompromising German policy in the East,
all the independent political organizations were to be suppressed.
The first Ukrainian political body which was to suffer this fate
was the Ukrainian Exile government (UNR), with its center
at Paris and a branch in Warsaw.

Shortly after the German occupation of Warsaw in 1939,
several members of the UNR cabinet were arrested by the
Gestapo. Among them were Prof. Roman Smal-Stocki, minister
of culture, and General Paul Shandruk, chief of staff of the UNR
army.

The Paris branch of UNR met a similar fate shortly after
that city passed under Nazi occupation. On Sept. 26, 1940, its
offices and archives were seized by the Gestapo, and the foreign
minister of UNR, Alexander Shulhyn, who headed the Paris
center, was arrested.

Only those members of UNR who resigned, abandoned their
independent course, and agreed to cooperate with the Germans
were spared. To this group belonged President Andrew Livytskyi who was used for propaganda purposes by Alfred Rosenberg's staff. Neither Andrew Livytskyi nor his followers had
any influence in Nazi-occupied Ukraine.[14]

Nazi authorities in Ukraine were especially eager to suppress

---

[13] *Ibid*, p 583 See also *Trial of War Criminals*, XXVII, 64-69
[14] Based on personal interviews and correspondence with members of the
UNR government

the political activity of two Ukrainian Nationalist organizations, OUN-B and OUN-M.[15] The two top leaders of those organizations, Stephan Bandera and Col. Andrew Melnyk, were confined to Berlin under a strict police surveillance shortly after the beginning of the Eastern campaign. On Sept. 15, 1941, Stephan Bandera and many of his principal lieutenants were incarcerated in the German concentration camp, Sachsenhausen. Col. Melnyk and his most prominent followers joined the "Banderivtsi" in the same concentration camp three years later on Jan. 26, 1944.[16] Meanwhile, the Gestapo conducted mass arrests and mass executions of the rank and file of the nationalist organizations in Ukraine. One of the first targets of German attack were the "task groups," organized by OUN-B and OUN-M in their Western European bases. These "task groups," which entered Ukraine with the German Wehrmacht or followed closely behind it, were supposed to spread the nationalist propaganda and to help to set up a new Ukrainian administration. Several of these civilian "task groups" were apprehended by German police in Balta, Nykolayev, Dzankoi (located in the Crimean Peninsula), Vasylkiv, and Fastiv, and their members were either executed or dispersed.[17]

The two military formations, called "Roland" and "Nachtigall," which were organized by OUN-B in cooperation with "Abwehr,"[18] were apprehended by Nazi authorities in Vynnytsia and near Tyraspol shortly after proclamation of Ukrainian independence in Lviv, and following the arrest of the Ukrainian Provisional government in this city; they were reorganized into a police unit and sent from Ukraine to Byelo-Russia to fight the Red partisans.[19] In the later stage of German occupation, this

[15] OUN-B also known as Banderivtsi or Revolutionary OUN led by Stephan Bandera, was a split group of the regular OUN under the leadership of Col. A Melnyk, it came into existence in exile one year before the beginning of the Eastern campaign. OUN-M or Melnykivtsi was the remainder of the old OUN under the leadership of Col A. Melnyk. This faction was more conservative in its outlook and more moderate in its tactics Both factions were involved in mutual feuds during most of German occupation though they amalgamated *de facto* their armed forces in the summer of 1943 in a common struggle against the Germans

[16] John Armstrong, *Ukrainian Nationalism 1939-1945* (New York Columbia University Press, 1955), p 177

[17] Matla, Zynoviy, *Pivdenna Pokhdina Hrupa* [The Southern Task Force], (Munich Cicero, 1952) See also J Armstrong, *op. cit.,* p 97

[18] Abwehr—the name of German military counter-intelligence service headed by Admiral Canaris

[19] Liubomyr Ortyns'kyi, *Druzhyny Ukrains'kykh Natsionalistiv (DUN).* [The Brotherhoods of Ukrainian Nationalists (OUN)], *Visti Bratstva kol. Voiakiv 1 UD UNA* (June-July, 1952). See also Armstrong, *op. cit.,* pp 74 and 153.

police unit joined the Ukrainian Insurgent army.[20]

The first blow against the adherents of the OUN-M organization was struck at the end of November, 1941, when the Melnyk adherents organized a big political rally to celebrate the anniversary of the execution of several hundred Ukrainian anti-Soviet partisans killed by the Red authorities at the close of the Civil war near the little town of Bazar. Two dozen of the organizers of this rally were executed by the Gestapo in Zhytomyr.[21] The next German step was the destruction of the OUN-M literary circle in Kiev. In the process of this action, several outstanding Ukrainian intellectuals such as the poetess, Olena Teliha; archeologist, Dr. Kandyba; and the journalist, John Rohach, were either arrested or executed. Their publications, such as the widely circulated daily, *Ukrainske Slowo* (Ukrainian Voice), and the literary magazine, *Litavry*, were suppressed. The Kievan press was turned over to the pro-Russian faction, which followed the German orders blindly.[22] The Germans then proceeded to purge the local Ukrainian administration, police, and press of nationalist adherents. Among others, they liquidated the mayors of Kiev, Poltava, and Kamenets-Podilskyi for alleged cooperation with the nationalists.[23]

In spite of these measures taken by German authorities in Ukraine against Ukrainian nationalist organizations, the Germans possessed an inadequate policing force to crush them completely. The German policy resulted only in driving these organizations deeper underground and in diverting their dynamic activity, which was mainly concerned with elimination of the remnants of the Soviet-Russian influences, directly against them. Even if German suppression of Ukrainian nationalist organizations is easily understandable in terms of the long-range German *Lebensraum* policy in Ukraine, the timing of such action was premature. The united German frontal attack against the Ukrainian nationalist rival parties as well as against the Ukrainian masses helped to bring about a united all-Ukrainian, anti-

[20] Ivan Krypyakevych et al , *History of the Ukrainian Armed Forces*, (Winnipeg· Ivan Tyktor, 1953), p 660.
[21] P. Dub, "V rokovyny demonstratsiyi v Bazari (spomyn)" [on the Anniversary of the Demonstration in Bazar (in Memoriam)], *Za Samostiynist* (November, 1946), pp 8-11 See also *OUN u Vyni* [The OUN in the War], Information Section of the OUN (UNR), (April, 1946), pp. 69-72, and Armstrong, *op. cit.*, p 107.
[22] Armstrong, *op. cit* , p 111.
[23] *Ibid* , p. 215.

German front which found its expression in the Ukrainian Insurgent army.

The German "Cassandra Calls" from the East

As long as the spectacular German military successes continued, Hitler's policy was acceptable to all Germans. But when the campaign in the East became prolonged and when it became clear that the Germans were being pushed back for the first time and when the weaknesses of the German military power was revealed for the first time, the possibility of utilizing popular political support was considered. The demand for German conciliation of the local populations grew stronger when Hitler's ruthless policy tended to prevent rather than to promote victory. The first issue concerned the prisoners of war, the number of whom strikingly diminished after the first news about the German treatment of them spread throughout the Red army. In the spring of 1942, Rosenberg mentioned in a letter to Keitel the effect that the policy of mass starvation had on Soviet prisoners of war in the German camps:

> We can say without exaggeration, that the mistake in treatment of prisoners of war is responsible to a great degree for the stiffening of resistance of the Red army and therefore also for the death of thousands of German soldiers.[24]

The stiffening of Red army resistence was not the only factor which jeopardized German chances for victory in Eastern Europe. Of vital importance was the attitude of the population in German-occupied Eastern Europe. Because neither German military nor civilian occupation authorities possessed sufficient police to enforce obedience or the ability to win the loyalty of millions of Russians, Ukrainians, and Byelo-Russians, the problem of securing food and raw materials from the occupied areas became extremely difficult. Moreover, the security of the military supply lines which stretched a thousand miles between Germany and the Eastern front became a matter of great concern. In spite of this fact, German policy in Eastern Europe continued to be harsh and absolutely uncompromising. This policy repelled every national group and every class in Eastern Europe. Justifying their policy, Himmler and Koch often said that they used the same means of force and oppression which

[24] *Trial of War Criminals*, XXV, 156

the Soviets had applied with apparent success for more than twenty years. This comparison was false. The Soviets never used such far-reaching and harsh measures toward whole populations, and they certainly did not apply these measures in time of war. To the contrary, the Soviet government adopted many pseudo-liberal reforms during World War II; for example, religious freedom was restored, national republics were granted the right to establish embassies, and many concentration camps were dissolved, the inmates of which were given a chance to fight for the "Fatherland." Red partisans promoted whispering campaigns, saying that Stalin planned the abolition of the kolchose system immediately after the war. At least the Soviets held an illusory prospect for a better future, while the Germans offered no ideology and no program for the Eastern nations but continued a policy of extermination or rule by force. There are many examples of statements revealing the lack of constructive policies on the part of the Germans. In point is the following command to German administrators in the East: "We do not want to turn Russians to National Socialism; all we want is to turn them into our working tools."[25]

Certainly, the Soviets were responsible for many mass executions and for enslavement measures directed against political prisoners and "hostile classes," but they never publicly displayed their violence. There were no public executions, no public floggings, or any kind of public violence. If arrests were made and people were deported, and there were many instances of this, the Soviets tried to bring them about in secret. If an individual was publicly condemned, the Soviets were always able to present his public repentance or incriminating self-confession.

The Germans, on the other hand, made a public show of force and violence, displaying cynical brutality and making no attempt to justify it on moral grounds.

In general, German policy in the East left the population no choice but to fight back. Some were converted to Communism as a lesser evil. The Soviet regime seemed, at least in its external form, to be more "liberal" in that it provided schools, cultural institutions, and granted formal equality. Many others—especially in Ukraine and in the Baltic states—realizing the mortal danger from both regimes, joined the ranks of their own nation-

[25] *Ibid.*, Doc O-89-USSR, sec. 8.

alist organizations and fought both Germans and Soviets. Some top German leaders were well aware of the dangerous growth of anti-German forces in the huge area in back of the Eastern front. Goebbels comments in his *Diary* in March, 1942:

> The partisans are in command of large areas in occupied Russia and are conducting a reign of terror there. The national movements, too, have become more insolent than it was at first imagined. That applies as well to the Baltic states as to Ukraine.[26]

As the dangers from anti-German forces grew and outbursts of large-scale partisan warfare seemed likely, the more realistic and intelligent German administrators and observers in the East became alarmed. They urged a revision of German Eastern policy. Such a point of view is expressed in a political report from Kiev, prepared by a professor of the German university in Posen, P. W. Thompson, dated Oct. 19, 1942:

> In this hour of decision for our people every fault may cause disastrous results. We can master the Polish and Czech problem; we can break them down because their populations are small. Small national groups such as the Estonians, Latvians, Lithuanians have to follow us or be annihilated.
>
> Quite different are circumstances in the huge Russian area, which we badly need as a raw material source. Without the cooperation of native people such as the White Ruthenians, Ukrainians, or the Russians we are not able to dominate those areas.[27]

Under these circumstances, Ukraine seemed to be a vital territory for a successful maintenance of the German Eastern front. Besides being the most important link connecting the German Eastern front with the Black Sea and with three German allies—Rumania, Hungary, and Slovakia. It was also the area through which Rumanian oil must flow to the Eastern front. It is quite understandable why the change from an initial friendly Ukrainian attitude to an anti-German outburst caused uneasiness among German experts on the East. A member of the Political Department of *Ostministerium* and former German consul in the Soviet Union, Otto Braeutigam, warned of the developments in Ukraine in a report dated Oct. 25, 1942:

[26] *The Goebbels Diaries*, p. 114.
[27] *Trial of War Criminals*, Doc. 303-PS.

Our policy of using Ukraine as a counterpoise against mighty Russia, against Poland and the Balkans and as a bridge to the Caucasus, was a complete failure. The forty million Ukrainians, who greeted us enthusiastically as liberators, are today quite indifferent to us and gravitate to the enemy's camp. If we do not succeed in checking this situation, we face, at the last moment, a danger that the Ukrainian partisan movement will be able to deny us Ukraine to a great extent as a source of food and to sever communication lines of the German army. Consequently its existence will be endangered, and the defeat of Germany will become imminent.[28]

These and similar warnings were not heeded either by Hitler or by his close associates. Hitler's policy of annihilation, enslavement, and national oppression continued until the inevitable happened. Early in 1943 in Northern Ukraine, large-scale anti-German partisan warfare began, and it soon swept through most of Ukraine.

The Vain Attempt

Anticipating military difficulties in the conquest and administration of the Soviet Union, two German groups wanted to take advantage of the political capital the Eastern campaign offered, which was reflected in the friendly attitude of the population and the many deserters, in order to reverse the political line followed by Hitler.

The first circle was formed around the *Ostministerium* and included Rosenberg, Braeutigam, and Professor von Mende, who was the leading German expert on Caucasian peoples. Another circle was formed in the German army, with its center on the Middle-Eastern front, and included such persons as Graf Staufenberg,[29] General Gehlen,[30] and General Koestring.[31] The first group stressed the importance of granting political freedom to the non-Russian nations, especially to Ukraine. And it urged a policy of moderation in these areas. This group was also known for its hostile attitude toward Great Russia. The German

---

[28] *Ibid*, Doc 294-PS (Secret note by Braeutigam, concerning the triple objective of the Eastern campaign and the general situation in the USSR).

[29] One of the managers of the Organization Department in the German General Staff, he was also the man who planted the bomb in Hitler's headquarters on July 20, 1944

[30] Head of the Department of German "Foreign Troops."

[31] The last German military attache in Moscow, in the year 1944, chief of Eastern European Military Formations on the German side.

military group was pro-Great Russia and was mostly interested in increasing the number of Russian deserters, saving Soviet prisoners of war from starvation, and organizing them in anti-Soviet military units.

The importance of using Russian prisoners in fighting the Soviets increased considerably after the Germans captured General Vlassov, who was head of a Russian Liberation committee. His appeals to the Red army called on the Soviet soldiers to join the Russian Liberation army on the German side. This brought a large number of Soviet deserters to the German ranks.[32] His German sponsors wanted to grant real authority to the Russian Liberation committee, and they also wanted to organize a Russian Liberation army under Vlassov's command. But Hitler constantly rejected such proposals as interfering with his Eastern policy.[33] As long as the Germans occupied Eastern Europe, Vlassov and his Russian Liberation committee were a fiction used for propaganda purposes behind and in the Soviet lines.[34] In the summer of 1944, when the great invasions began in Normandy and when the Eastern front was being pushed westward toward the German boundaries, Himmler—a bitter enemy of the Vlassov movement—changed his mind partially and supported the idea of Vlassov's Russian Liberation army.[35] He also supported the Great Russian conception of Vlassov and placed all non-Russian voluntary formations from the East under Vlassov. Initially, these troops were created from units of Eastern European deserters which had been scattered throughout the German army and in Eastern European formations of the SS troops. Their size varied from division to company. Some smaller Eastern European units were organized by the Wehrmacht in 1941 and increased steadily in spite of Hitler's restrictive orders against such measures. Larger military groups, usually of division size, were built at the beginning of 1943 on the initiative of younger SS officers in "SS-Hauptamt" (Gruppe Sparkmann).[36] At the time Himmler decided to form a Russian Liberation army, the number of Eastern European troops in the German army amounted to an impressive total of 900,000 to 1,000,000.[37]

---

[32] *Development of State, op. cit*, (Summer, 1954), No. 2 (13), p. 26.
[33] *Ibid*, p. 27
[34] *Ibid*
[35] Thorwald, *op cit.,* p. 378-379.
[36] *Ibid*, pp. 327-331.
[37] *Ibid.,* p. 410.

Himmler's attempt to subordinate the non-Russian voluntary troops and their National committees to the command of Vlassov met with obstinate resistance from soldiers of all nationalities.[38] The importance of this resistance is revealed in the number of people involved. The number of non-Russian and non-German troops in the Eastern European formations in October, 1944, was:

Ukrainians	220,000[39]
Turkenstanians	110,000
Caucasians	110,000
Tartars	35,000
Cossacks	82,000
Lithuanians	27,000
Latvians	3 SS divisions
Estonians	2 SS divisions
Kalmycks	29 squadrons
Byelo-Russians	1 SS division[40]

Totaling more than 600,000, they formed an overwhelming force when compared to the 300,000 to 400,000 Russians who were loyal to Vlassov. The real amalgamation of those nationalities with Vlassov forces never occurred although the Gestapo pressed for it and even threatened different national leaders to get them to accept Vlassov's leadership.[41] Over a period of time, the concept of national independence rather than subordination to Russia seemed to win even the hard heads of German Gestapo leaders. At least, the Ukrainian Liberation committee was recognized by the Germans as an independent body on March 15, 1945, not quite two months before the German capitulation.[42]

Organization by the Germans of anti-Soviet formations from the large Eastern European reservoir came too late and at a time when most of the psychological factors favorable to success were gone. The only asset which the Germans possessed until the end was the fear of Bolshevism which induced many former subjects of the Soviet Union to fight on the German side. Their number proves the potentiality of the anti-Soviet forces in the Soviet Union, a strength not utilized because of Hitler's policy.

[38] *Ibid.*, p. 415.
[39] P. Shandruk, "It Was This Way," in *Development of State*, No. 3 (14), (Autumn, 1954)
[40] Kleist, *Zwischen Hitler und Stalin*, p. 205.
[41] Thorwald, *op. cit.*, pp. 422-424.
[42] *Development of State, op. cit.*, p. 40.

German Lebensraum Ueber Alles

An analysis of German political mistakes in Eastern Europe must include another crucial point. Why did Hitler fail to reverse his suicidal policy in the East until he had completely lost these territories and until it was too late? To understand his attitude, one must understand not only his fanatical adherence to his ideology but one must also realize that the main objective of his foreign policy was to secure the German *Lebensraum* in the East.[43] Hitler viewed such a policy as the only possible way in which to make the German nation both great and healthy. The most explicit evidence of the importance of this idea to Hitler may be perceived from his interview with Peter Kleist, the leading official in *Ostministerium*. Kleist tried to induce the Fuehrer to revise his policy in Eastern Europe. He presented the most convincing facts concerning the deteriorating effect of this policy on the German position in Eastern Europe. In this interview, which took place in the summer of 1943, Hitler rejected a proposed revision of his policy.

The German people will become, in a hundred years, a Nation of 120 millions. For this people I need an empty space. I cannot grant sovereign rights to the Soviet peoples, and I cannot set up in place of Soviet Russia a new national and therefore strongly united Russia. Politics is made not by illusions but by hard facts. The space problem is the most decisive factor for me in the East.[44]

Similar stress on the need of East European space for the Third Reich was expressed by Himmler. In a speech to his SS men in Posen on Oct. 14, 1943, he said:

For us the end of war seems a free way to the East, the creation of a Teutonic Empire and of securing in one way or another—how we cannot now say—30 millions people of our blood, so that within our lifetime we will become a Nation of 120 millions Teutons.[45]

How far eastward the Nazis wanted to extend their "Teutonic Empire" is not known. It is doubtful if Hitler wanted to include within German territory the whole of ethnographic Russia or to eliminate Russia completely as a state. There are, however, some indications that he wanted to make Russia mili-

[43] Hitler, *op cit*, p 654.
[44] Kleist, *Zwischen Hitler und Stalin*, pp. 224-225.
[45] *Trial of War Criminals*, XXXVII, 523.

tarily and biologically impotent so as to prevent any future attempt to recover the territories which Germany wanted to occupy. The desired territory was first of all Ukraine. Ribbentrop hinted at some aspects of future German policy toward Russia in a talk with Italian Foreign Minister Bastianini during April, 1943:

> For in any case the Russian problem may find only a military solution but no sudden political solution. Germany cannot leave the Russians close to the German boundary without being exposed to the danger of an air attack one day. Besides, Germany needs Ukraine. Already, as I mentioned before, we have annihilated 14 millions Russians. One day the population of Russia will be so scarce that she will present no danger any more.[46]

There can be no doubt, however, that the whole of Ukraine was supposed to be included in the German *Lebensraum* and that it was intended to be the most essential part. Germans always seemed to emphasize this point and sometimes stated bluntly that Ukraine was one of the most important targets of their aggressive actions. The former American consul in Berlin, Raymond H. Geist, recalls his talks with leading Nazi leaders:

> In December, 1938, I had a conversation with General Franz Halder, who was then Chief of Staff, at the house of Dr. Etscheit, a prominent Berlin lawyer. Halder stated to me: "You must take into account the National Socialist program in the East If you, the Western Powers, oppose our program in the East, we shall have to go to war with you."
>
> During this conversation he made clear to me that the program of the Nazis for expansion in the East, was unalterably fixed and decided upon. It included the attack on Poland, the annexation of Austria, territorial expansion in Yugoslavia, Czechoslovakia, Rumania, and Russia, particularly in Ukraine. The latter provinces would have to be German.[47]

No less revealing were the words of the Fuehrer when he related Ukraine to his war aims during a conference with Field-marshal Keitel[48] and General Zeitzler[49] in Berghof on Aug. 6, 1943. During this conference, he said:

---

[46] *Ibid*, XXXV, 444-445.
[47] *Ibid*, XXVIII, 239.
[48] Wilhelm Keitel, Chief of Supreme Command of German Army.
[49] Kurt Zeitzler, Chief of German General Staff.

The only decisive thing is that we should not suc-
cumb to the influences which say: Maybe once in an ad-
verse situation there will be only one thing left over—
to create an Ukrainian State. Then everything will be in
order, then we shall get a million soldiers. We shall get
not a single soldier! It is only an illusion the same as it
was in the First World War. Doing this we committed
the greatest self-delusion. Indeed, we would resign from
all the objectives of this war.[50]

As can be seen, the main purpose and meaning of the war
to Hitler and to his closest associates such as Himmler and Koch
was territorial expansion and the colonization of Germans in
Eastern Europe. In the colonization scheme, Ukraine occupied
a key position, and Poland, the Baltic states, and Byelo-Russia
were to be included in the German *Lebensraum* more or less
as territories which would link Germany to Ukraine.

These countries were put under a direct German administration unlike all of the other European countries conquered by
Hitler. Other states were permitted a semblance of independence even though they remained vassal states. Vichy France,
Nedic's Serbia, Pavelic's Croatia, and Quisling's Norway were
given vassal governments ruled by their own nationals. The
purpose of this clear-cut difference in policy is obvious. In the
Eastern European countries, Hitler wanted German colonies,
and he planned to incorporate them fully into Germany. Hitler
planned to deal with the second category of countries as well
as with the German allies and the few remaining neutral countries in two different ways: a) The Germanic countries such as
Norway, Denmark, Sweden, and Holland should be integrated
with Germany, and their population should supply settlers for
the Eastern *Lebensraum;*[51] b) as for the rest of Europe, Hitler
planned to keep it under German hegemony[52] and to organize it
in a security system in a form of a "New Europe," which would
support and defend his policy in Eastern Europe.

---

[50] *Development of State, op. cit.,* (Summer, 1954), No 2 (13), sec. *Doc.*
[51] Picker, *op. cit.,* p. 19.
[52] *Ibid ,* p. 44.

U. P. A. Activity

CHAPTER 5

PARTISAN WARFARE IN UKRAINE, 1941-1944

A great contribution to the victory over Germany was made by you, the Ukrainian Insurgents. You prevented the German's ruling at his free will on Ukrainian soil and exploiting it for his imperialistic purposes. You prevented him from robbing Ukrainian villages, and you prevented deportations to Germany. Your punishing hand revenged properly for the shooting and burning of villages. In the struggle against Germany, our Ukrainian Insurgent army passed through its first school of combat.[1]

The Ukrainian ally turned into an enemy. The Nationalist Ukrainian Organization (OUN) went over to the opposition, and with the passage of time there was created an Ukrainian Resistance army (UPA).[2]

The Initial Stage of Warfare and German Reaction

THE ANTI-GERMAN partisan warfare in Ukraine may be subdivided roughly into two types: a) That which was conducted by the militarily trained, specialized, small groups, and b) the larger and heterogeneous partisan detachments which arose through the spontaneous participation of the population. The first type of warfare began with the very outbreak of German-Soviet hostilities. It was conducted, on order of the Soviet authorities, by special military groups which infiltrated or were parachuted behind German lines, or by isolated groups which still survived the rapid German advance eastward. This early Soviet partisan warfare was limited and not very successful because of the low morale of the Red army at the beginning of the war and because of the lack of popular support which is essential to any partisan warfare. As late as March 16, 1943, the Reichskommissar of Ukraine, Erich Koch, wrote with satisfaction:

[1] Ivan Krypyakevych, et al., *The History of the Ukrainian Armed Forces,* 2nd. rev ed , Gen. Taras Chuprynka from Orders to UPA, May, 1945, (Winnipeg: Myron Levytsky, 1953), p. 650.
[2] Peter Kleist, *Zwischen Hitler und Stalin,* p. 190.

Concerning the behavior of the Ukrainians: They are, fortunately, passive *en masse*. In the liquidation of the Bolshevik bands, they help neither the Bolsheviks nor the German police.[3]

The gulf which existed between the Communist professional partisan groups and the population of Ukraine was partially closed by German reaction to partisan warfare in Eastern Europe. The determining factor in this connection was the will of the Fuehrer who expressed his thoughts concerning this topic on July 16, 1941:

The Russians now have an order for a partisan warfare behind our lines. This partisan warfare also has its advantages. It gives us the chance to eliminate everybody who is against us.[4]

Hitler's policy was to use partisan warfare conducted by the Soviets as an excuse for the elimination of hostile elements in Eastern Europe. This policy might have been successful in eliminating the intellectual groups in Eastern Europe, which were partially under German control and which the Germans regarded as a self-conscious independent element, but it extended rather than limited partisan warfare. The secret order issued by Keitel on Sept. 16, 1941, to the German troops on the Eastern front commanded shooting of fifty to one hundred hostages for the killing of a single German soldier.[5] Suffering German retaliation for deeds which they did not commit, the population had only two alternatives—either to seek the protection of the Red partisans or to form their own protective partisan groups. Seeing through the German tactics, Red partisans often used these tactics to their advantage. They would kill a few Germans here and there, disrupt the German communications lines and then retreat rapidly, exposing the population to the rage of German retaliation in order to increase their following or to punish some anti-Soviet villagers.[6] Similar tactics frequently were used by Red partisans against the partisan groups who independently fought the Germans.[7] When the harshness of the German occupation increased and the popula-

[3] *Trial of War Criminals*, Doc 192-PS. Letter of Reichskommissar of Ukraine, Erich Koch, to Minister for the East, Alfred Rosenberg
[4] *Ibid*, Doc 221-L File memorandum from July 16, 1941, on a discussion by Hitler with Rosenberg, Lammers, Keitel, and Goering
[5] *Ibid*, Doc 389-PS Keitel's top-secret directive
[6] Krypyakevych, et al , *op. cit* , p. 657
[7] *Ibid*, p 676, cited from D Medvedev, *Those of Strong Spirit*, (Moscow Voyennoye izdat , 1951), p 293

tion of Ukraine was driven to the point of desperation, a mass partisan movement of national character began which was hostile to the German as well as to the Soviet regime.

The Origin and Purpose of the Non-Soviet Partisan Groups

Non-Soviet partisan warfare in Ukraine went back to four different origins: (a) The group of Otaman Bulba-Borovets; (b) Ukrainian Nationalist Organization branch under the leadership of Colonel Andrew Melnyk; (c) Ukrainian Nationalist Organization branch under the leadership of Stephen Bandera, and (d) the Polish underground.

The partisan group, under Otaman Bulba-Borovets, was organized in the northwestern Ukrainian province of Volynia before the outbreak of the German-Russian war in 1940.[8] The purpose of this group was to organize an anti-Bolshevik uprising. After the outbreak of the Soviet-German war, Bulba led an autonomous partisan detachment and fought the Red army in Eastern Polissya. When the blunt German attitude toward Ukrainian independence became apparent, Bulba's group again went underground and fought against the Germans as early as February, 1942. Bulba's detachment—a force of 150 to 300 men[9]—operated in the District of Ludwipol, near Rowno, and also in the Districts of Sarny and Kostopil, along the Sluch River. Bulba's troops were the first to call themselves "The Ukrainian Insurgent Army (UPA)."

Melnyk's branch of the Ukrainian Nationalist Organization (OPN) maintained two partisan training camps in Volynia, one south of the town of Kremyanec and another in the vicinity of the town of Volodymyr.[10] The OUN, under the leadership of Bandera, organized a partisan detachment in October, 1942, in Polissya, in the province which lies north of Volynia. The Bandera branch of the OUN proved to be the most effective among all the existing Ukrainian partisan groups. During the autumn of 1942 and the spring of 1943, it multiplied with amazing rapidity and emerged with considerable military strength. Early in the year 1943, it started negotiations with the other Ukrainian National insurgent groups. The negotiations

[8] Petro Mirchuk, *The Ukrainian Insurgent Army 1942-1952*, (Munich Cicero, 1953), p 63

[9] Krypyakevych, et al , *op cit* , p 659.

[10] *Ibid* , p 658

failed because of the problems of personal leadership. This failure led finally to a forceful amalgamation of Bulba's and Melnyk's detachments, strengthened by the OUN branch under the leadership of Bandera.[11]

The partisan movements in Ukraine were by no means homogeneous either in their origin or in their ultimate goals. The Soviet partisans were sent into action, equipped, and directed by Moscow. Their main purpose was the disruption of the German lines of communication and military intelligence, and the preparation of the way for the Red army. Their strength was based on superior military training and equipment. Their weakness was their lack of general popular support, because they represented a government which was not only feared but hated. The villages of Ukraine must have remembered the horrors of the compulsory collectivization which had many qualities similar to the ruthlessness of the German administration. Still the formerly small and specialized Red partisan detachments increased considerably during the period of the spontaneous partisan movement.[12] Sometimes the population was forcibly mobilized by the Red partisans. Many others joined the Red partisans fearing that with the advance of the Red army they would be labeled as traitors for having remained under the German occupation and that joining the Red partisans would be the only chance to prove their loyalty.

The ultimate purpose of the Ukrainian Insurgent army was an Independent Ukrainian state; their immediate task was the protection of the Ukrainian population against the most abusive forms of German colonial policy. Their strength was the popular support in Ukraine, due mainly to the fact that they declared war against both the German and Soviet regimes. Another strong point was the idea which they preached. "Liberty to men and freedom to the nations." This set them above the narrow nationalists. This call secured them not only the cooperation of all classes in Ukraine but also the cooperation and support of many nationals such as Slovaks, Jews, Georgians, and Tartars.[13] Their weakness was their international position. None of the great powers, Germany, the Soviet Union, or the Western Allies, would or could sympathize with their ultimate goal. Consequently, arms, military training, and leadership had to be

[11] Mirchuk, *op cit.*, p. 62-64
[12] Krypyakevych, et al , *op. cit.*, p. 661.
[13] Mirchuk, *op. cit* , pp. 69-72.

obtained on their own. This was one of the reasons why the first of the numerous detachments of the Ukrainian National partisans appeared in the spring of 1943, almost two years after the beginning of the German occupation.[14]

The purpose of the Polish underground, which was limited to the northwestern part of Ukraine (provinces which belonged until 1939 to Poland), was to prepare for the restoration of Polish rule. The strength of the Polish underground was its ties with the Polish underground movements in Poland proper, e.g., with "Home Army" and "National Armed Forces" (N.S.T.). Both organizations supplied the Polish underground in Ukraine with arms and trained leaders, part of which they in turn obtained from the Western Allies.

The fact that Poland was a faithful partner of the Western Allies and that the Polish-Soviet treaty of August, 1941,[15] nullified the Soviet-German treaty on behalf of Poland from 1939 on, encouraged the Polish underground and the Polish minorities to behave in the mentioned provinces as the future masters. The Common Defense treaty[16] which the Polish Exile government concluded with the Soviet Union on Dec. 4, 1941, resulted in cooperation between the Polish and Soviet undergrounds. Both the Polish underground and the Polish population in Ukraine were inclined to regard the Red partisans and the advancing Red army as their actual or at least temporary allies.[17] This and the above mentioned behavior of the Poles contributed strongly toward Polish-Ukrainian feuds under German occupation. The weakness of the Polish underground in Ukraine was its dispersion and isolation in the sea of a Ukrainian population which was bitterly hostile to the idea of a new annexation to Poland and therefore highly antagonistic to the Polish appeals for cooperation.[18]

Growth and Extension of the Ukrainian National Partisan Movement

Spontaneous partisan warfare began in Ukraine in the spring of 1943, and it rapidly increased the ranks of the Ukrainian

---

[14] *Ibid.*, pp. 25-26
[15] *Interior Policy of USSR During the Period of the Fatherland War, Documents and Materials*, (Moscow Ogiz, 1946), I, pp 137-138.
[16] *Ibid*, I, p 191
[17] *Polskie Siły Zbrojne w Drugiej Wojnie Swiatowej* [Polish Armed Forces During W.W. II, Vol III, Home Army], (London: Instytut im. Gen. Sikorskiego), p 584.
[18] *Ibid.*, pp 584-85

Insurgent army. Many of its locally based "Home Protective Detachments" were transformed into aggressive fast moving troops, who often covered hundreds of miles in their raids against the Germans. With their training and supply bases safely entrenched in the barely accessible marshes of Polissya, in the forests of Volynia, and in the Carpathian Mountains, they started their operations in those provinces. The first attack against the Germans by the First Company of UPA occurred on Feb. 7, 1943. During this action, the UPA forces conquered the town of Volodymyrec, destroyed the local German police station, and annihilated a detachment of German police and a detachment of Cossacks in the German service.[19] In the next month, UPA could record such events as a raid on an arms and ammunition factory in the town of Orshev, the conquest of the country town of Olyka, a raid on the war prisoner camp in Luck, and the liberation of war and political prisoners from the jail and camps in the city of Kowel.[20] The conditions in the provinces of Volynia and Polissya in the spring of 1943 are described by Prof. L. Shankovsky as follows:

> In the first half of April, 1943, the Ukrainian Insurgent movement dominated Volynia and a considerable part of Polissya. The Germans asserted themselves only in the larger towns and townships where they created strongholds with the help of formidable garrisons. They were busy also with the protection of the railway lines supplying the Eastern front. These supply lines were also protected by the pill-boxes manned with the Hungarian troops and patrolled by the armored trains. The Volynian highroads were steadily patrolled by the armored cars.[21]

German protection of their supply and communication lines was not sufficient, however This was soon proved when a detachment of the UPA, called "Revenge of Polissya," succeeded in killing the chief of German SA, Victor Lutze, on the highroad between Kowel and Brest Litowsk early in May of 1943.[22] Soon the German supply lines in Ukraine became even more vulnerable. In July of 1943 came reports of the UPA success in capturing a German military train near the station at Manevychi (Volynia), of a victorious raid on a motorized German military

[19] Krypyakevych, et al., *op. cit.*, p. 662.
[20] *Ibid*, p. 662.
[21] *Ibid*, p. 662
[22] *Ibid*, p. 665.

column on the highroad from Radomysl to Koczereve (near Kiev), and of a fight for the railway station of Ivnycia on the railroad line from Khvastiv to Zhytomyr.[23] A secret report written in June, 1943, by German Commissioner General Leyser indicates the impact which partisan warfare had on the German lines of communication:

> On behalf of the bands' activities . . . I could only say that the situation grows worse from day to day. . . . Only a single road in the General District, that from Zhytomyr to Vinnitsa, is passable without an armed escort. However, as the bands' activity spreads now toward the south, it is probable that we shall soon be compelled to introduce an escort system also on this single road. All other roads . . . are passable only with ready-to-fire guns and machine guns.[24]

In the summer of 1943, the activity of the UPA extended also to Southern Ukraine. There were two local Ukrainian partisan detachments operating in Southern Ukraine—one in the Uman area and another in the large forested area called Kholodnyi Yar.[25] These two detachments were strengthened by fresh troops sent from the provinces of Volynia and Polissya, all of which were combined into one unified army group called the UPA-South. In the autumn of 1943, the UPA-South operated in the areas of Haisyn, Lityn, Yatychiv, and Zhmerynka. Among its major anti-German operations were an encounter with German police near the village of Semyduby (District of Uman), and the liquidation of a German police station in the county town of Lityn.[26]

The Beginning of Partisan Warfare in Western Ukraine

Western Ukraine which was incorporated by the Germans into the General Government under the name of District of Galizien was free of any significant partisan activities until the summer of 1943. This fact seems strange when one considers that this region was known as the stronghold of Ukrainian nationalism and was often referred to as the Piedmont of Ukraine. Therefore, consideration should be given to what

[23] *Ibid*, pp. 673, 678-9.
[24] *Trial of War Criminals*, Doc 265-PS.
[25] Krypyakevych, et al., *op cit.*, p 681.
[26] *Ibid.*, p. 682.

factors there were in play and to what explanation can be found
for this strange phenomenon. Professor L. Shankovsky, who
has studied the history of the Ukrainian Insurgent army, explains
that the lack of partisan actions in this area was a deliberate
plan of the UPA. According to him, the high command of the
UPA wanted to have the District of Galizien free of any partisan
activity in Western Ukraine in order to be undisturbed here in
their efforts to collect supplies and to train soldiers and officers
for fighting in other areas of Ukraine.[27] This explanation is inadequate because it assumes that the command of the UPA had a
free hand to decide where partisan warfare should or should not
be conducted. But the facts indicate that freedom of action was
rather limited. It has been noted that the growth of the UPA
coincided with the growth of spontaneous uprisings and that
the UPA more than any other partisan formation was dependent
upon popular support. Consequently, the UPA was to a great
degree dependent upon the needs and demands in the various
regions of Ukraine. It must be asked if the District of Galizien
suffered less from the German occupation, causing less popular
demand for anti-German warfare than in the other parts of
Ukraine. This question must be answered in the negative.
Although the Ukrainians in the District of Galizien had privi-
leges[28] which their brothers in Reichskommissariat Ukraine did
not enjoy, the basic German policy in Galizien was no less ruthless.[29] So one must look for other factors which brought about
the sentiment of the Ukrainian population in the District of
Galizien which was so different when compared to other parts
of Ukraine.

The only plausible explanation of the differing sentiment
in the District of Galizien may be in the fact that early in the
spring the Germans started the formation of a voluntary SS-
Division Galizien from Western Ukrainian population. On this
occasion, Western Ukrainian representatives were able to win
some concessions in return for Ukrainian participation in this
project. The concessions stipulated that the division should be
Ukrainian in character, that the Germans would liberate Ukrainian prisoners of war and political prisoners, and that the independence of Ukraine would be recognized by the Germans in

[27] *Ibid*, p 686
[28] The Ukrainians in the Western Ukraine were allowed to maintain a Central Aid committee which started a welfare program and opened a
   limited number of high schools
[29] *Trial of War Criminals*, Doc. 1526-PS.

the future.[30] The governor of the District of Galizien promised
to fulfill these conditions, and the enlistments for the division
proceeded successfully. This German move neutralized the
violent Ukrainian antagonism against the Germans in this special
region of Ukraine for some time. Some of the Ukrainians regarded the creation of the SS Division Galizien as the first step
toward the formation of the Ukrainian National army and consequently considered it as radical change of German policy
toward Ukraine.

The OUN, spiritual father of UPA, which feverishly worked
on the preparation of military cadres in Western Ukraine, continued to doubt the sincerity of German intentions toward
Ukraine and refused to cooperate with the Germans. Consequently, it opposed the formation of the Division Galizien
and conducted a strong campaign among Ukrainians against it.
But they could not prevent the formation of the unit. Public
opinion in Western Ukraine remained divided on this issue.
But the psychological factors were not favorable in the spring
of 1943 to conduct an extensive open action against the Germans
in Western Ukraine. Thus, it is easy to see why the UPA high
command concentrated its strength against the Germans in
Reichskommissariat Ukraine, where there were no doubts of
anti-Ukrainian German policy and the support of the population against the Germans was wholehearted.

It is a matter of speculation as to how the German-Ukrainian
agreements of the spring of 1943 would have lasted if external
factors had not interfered. It can be argued that it would not
have lasted long. The creation of SS Division Galizien was the
idea of the governor of the District of Galizien, Dr. Waechter,
and of a small group of young SS officers within the SS headquarters.[31] They had enough authority to create a Ukrainian
division, but they had neither power nor authority to change
the course of German policy toward the whole Ukraine or even
toward the one region. Consequently, no expected changes
occurred. Gestapo rule, which was higher than Governor Waechter and which had virtual control in Western Ukraine, was as
ruthless as it ever had been, and the future promised to be
worse. To make room for German colonists, Governor General
Frank, working closely with the Gestapo, planned a mass depor-

---

[30] Krypyakevych, et al., *op. cit*, p. 605.
[31] Thorwald, *op cit.*, pp 327-329.

tation of Ukrainians from many areas of Western Ukraine in the summer of 1943.[32] It was obvious that such mass deportation would lead to widespread resistance in Western Ukraine. This colonization plan of the Germans was not destined to succeed, and there were different and quite unexpected reasons which gave rise to anti-German partisan warfare in Western Ukraine.

Early in the summer of 1943, a large Red partisan group (3,000 to 5,000 men),[33] under the leadership of General Sydor Kovpak, penetrated the northwestern boundary of the District of Galizien and proceeded across country toward the Carpathian Mountains. Their goal was to destroy German oil refineries in the Western Ukrainian Carpathian region and then to occupy the Carpathian Mountain passes and to keep them under control in order to harass not only the German communication lines and the German administration of the northern side of the mountains but also to undermine morale and loyalty of German allies, Hungary and Slovakia, on the other side of the mountains. Kovpak's little army took the German administration in Western Ukraine by surprise. The Germans had insufficient forces in the region to oppose such an unexpected enemy. Kovpak's forces reached the Carpathian Mountains almost unopposed, killing and dispersing the German administration and police en route, pillaging and burning their stores of supplies, and destroying their communication lines and military constructions. Their attitude toward the population was correct, but because they had to supply themselves with food and clothing at the expense of the population, they caused mutual tensions. The cause of the tensions is so much more apparent when one considers the size of Kovpak's group and the shortage of food in the poverty-stricken mountain regions of Western Ukraine.

Further, the political attitude of the population was hostile to the Red partisans. The Kovpakovtsi posed at first as an advance guard of the Red army, and there was hardly anyone in Western Ukraine who did not recall the Red army occupation in the years 1939 to 1941 without a shudder. The OUN itself could not look with indifference on the settling of the Kovpak partisans in the Carpathian Mountains. Public opinion demanded action and defense against them, and the OUN had to respond to the sentiments of the population on which the success of their future actions depended. The OUN could not afford to

[32] *Trial of War Criminals*, XXIX, 605
[33] Krypyakevych, et al , *op. cit.*, p. 661.

lose its valuable supplies and training schools in the Carpathian Mountains without a fight. Therefore, the OUN, working with the population, organized defensive detachments called the Ukrainian Peoples Self-Defense (UNS).

In the meantime, the Germans mobilized troops, and after weeks of treacherous warfare they succeeded in encircling and destroying the main Kovpak forces. The smaller and splintered Kovpak detachments then started to withdraw toward the East, hampered by the troops of the UNS and a hostile population.[34] After the Carpathian Mountains were cleared of the Red partisans, Germans in Western Ukraine were faced by the Ukrainian National partisans whom they regarded as no less dangerous. For a short time, a delaying truce prevailed. Since the OUN would not disband its newly created army detachments and the Germans would not tolerate an independent force in the Carpathians which interfered with their policy, a clash was inevitable.

On Aug. 18, 1943, a detachment of the UNS attacked a German punitive labor camp near the town of Skole. German guards and personnel were killed, and the prisoners were freed.[35] Following this incident, skirmishes occurred near the towns of Skole, Kolomea, and near the Dnister River. In the latter part of September and in the first half of October, the Germans undertook several expeditions against the UNS training centers and their supply bases in the counties of Skole and Kolomea but met with no definite success and incurred heavy losses.[36] Heavy fighting between the Germans and the Ukrainian National partisans occurred during the autumn and winter of 1943-1944 on such a large scale that the OUN decided on Jan. 27, 1944, to organize an Insurgent army in Western Ukraine. In January, 1944, Western Ukraine partisan forces were strengthened by detachments sent from the provinces of Volynia and Polissya. All were organized into the UPA-Group-West.

In the early spring of 1944, the reorganized and strengthened Ukrainian partisan forces in Western Ukraine started an action against the large German-owned estates called *Liegenschaften*. The main goal of this action was to obtain food for the UPA

---

[34] For a detailed account of Kovpak's raid, study his book· Sydor Kovpak, *From Putywl to the Carpathian Mountains,* (Moscow-Leningrad: Gospolitizdat, 1946); and P. Vershygora: *The People With an Unstained Conscience* (Moscow: Sovetsky Pisatel, 1951)

[35] Mirchuk, *op cit* , p. 46.

[36] Krypyakevych, et al., *op. cit.,* p. 688.

forces. Thirty *Liegenschaften* in the county of Stanislaviv and almost all of them in the county of Kolomea were liquidated by the end of March, 1944.[37]

During the spring and summer of 1944 when the Soviet-German battle line ran across Western Ukraine and most of the German administration was withdrawn, the Ukrainian partisan warfare limited itself to securing all possible war supplies and arms from the retreating German army. Major encounters with German and Hungarian troops were conducted in the counties of Kolomea, Bolekhiv, Skole, and Turka, along the Carpathian Mountain chains. The goal of most of the fighting was to gain dominance of the mountain strongholds and of the German lines of supply and retreat. By the end of the summer of 1944, most of the Ukrainian territory was cleared of Germans, and the UPA turned its forces against a new enemy—the Soviet Union.

How Germans Tried to Check the Ukrainian National Insurgent Movement

German measures against the fighting partisan movements in Ukraine included direct military expeditions, a wave of terror directed against the entire population, and crude anti-partisan propaganda. German terror tactics included the shooting of political prisoners and hostages. This tactic was applied especially in Reichskommissariat Ukraine. In pursuing this policy early in 1943, the Germans executed the following: Feb. 23, 40 Ukrainian hostages killed in the city of Kremyanec (Volynia); and on March 8, 485 Ukrainian political prisoners shot in the jail of Rovno (capital of Reichskommissariat Ukraine).[38] In addition, the Germans extended their executions to the smaller villages. There were mass executions in villages which supplied or supported partisans. The Germans often punished villages through which the partisans merely passed. The punishment of the guilty was by no means the aim—the aim was terror. While pursuing the Kovpak group of Red partisans in Western Ukraine, German troops massacred the population of a mountain village, Bili Oslawy,[39] although there was no evidence that the population and the Red partisans had cooperated. Mass executions of village residents was a common practice of the Germans when

---

[37] *Ibid.*, p. 690.
[38] *Ibid*, p. 668
[39] *Ibid*, p 668.

conducting anti-guerilla warfare in the provinces of Volynia and Polissya. One example of the German tactics is the fate of the village of Remel (Alexandria county) where the Germans executed 600 people.[40] The village of Malyn (Ostroh county) is another terrifying example. Here, both buildings and inhabitants were burned by SS General Bach-Zelewsky, who was known as Himmler's specialist in fighting against bands. In this unfortunate village, 624 Czech colonists and 116 Ukrainian farmers lost their lives.[41] The military courts, which started on Oct. 10, 1943, were introduced by the Germans in the District of Galizien as an answer to Ukrainian partisan warfare. These courts condemned to death not only those involved in partisan movements but also those who were under suspicion for the slightest reason. The author, who lived at this time in Stanislaviv, second largest city of Western Ukraine, recalls that many foresters were executed in this city because partisan supply barracks were found in the forests under their administration. The author recalls also that his uncle, a Catholic priest, was hunted for months by the Gestapo for holding funeral rites over the bodies of partisans killed in a battle with the Germans. The Germans failed to realize that their methods of fighting the Ukrainian partisan movement did not create effective moral support for the regime but caused more of the young men and women to join the partisans.

German anti-partisan propaganda was based on four main points: 1) That the National partisans were indeed Red agents; 2) that the population who supported the National partisans would be punished at the Lord's Last Judgment; 3) that German arms were invincible; and 4) that Germany symbolized European culture and civilization. The first point was too absurd to be believed, the second point was ridiculous; the third point was at least very doubtful after the German debacle at Stalingrad; and the fourth point was completely refuted by barbarous Nazi behavior not only toward human beings but also against such cultural institutions as schools, museums, and libraries in Ukraine.[42] There was nothing the Germans could offer the population except eventual defeat of Communism and continuation of a German regime which was equally ruthless. The UPA, on

[40] *Ibid*, p 668.
[41] *Ibid*, p 672
[42] *Trial of War Criminals*, Doc 303-PS. Political report by Prof. Paul Thompson from Kiev, on Oct. 19, 1942.

the other hand, promised justice, human rights, free land, and an independent state. Physically, most of the village population was under German control only during occasional raids. Partisan control was in force for the rest of the time. To cooperate with the partisans meant possible German retaliation. But cooperation with the Germans meant certain death.

The Impact of Partisan Warfare on the German Occupation

Partisan control in some areas in Volynia, Polissya, and in the Carpathian region increased to such a degree that virtual "insurgent republics" were created.[43] In such areas, the partisans created their own governmental agencies to take care of the forest economy, to distribute the land to the farmers, and even to run the schools.[44] The effect of such partisan rule on the German economy may be learned from the secret report of General Commissioner Leyser from Zhytomyr, June 30, 1943:

> As a result of the extensive activity of the partisan bands, we possess control of only 40% of the land that was formerly cultivated regularly in our General District. Around 60% is under control of bands. The bands supply the population regularly with the growing crops and let the peasants cultivate the soil . . . with an apparent intention of reaping a harvest in the autumn. As a result of bands activity we control only the following percentages of the live stock: Cattle—36%, pigs—41%, ships—28%. Milk delivery was reduced to 42% and egg delivery to 51%. Also the forest economy causes us especial trouble. The General District of Zhytomyr is very rich in forests. But around 1,400,000 hectares of the forests, which means 80% of all forests in this District, are occupied by bands. . . .[45]

The only effective way for the Germans to fight the partisan movement in Ukraine while still maintaining their old policy was either by garrisoning the region or deporting the population. At this time the Germans did not possess the resources with which to carry out such measures on a large scale. And partisan warfare in Ukraine bound considerable German forces to Ukraine and was very expensive to them. In the big action in the summer of 1943, conducted by SS General Bach-Zelewsky

---

[43] Krypyakevych, et al., *op. cit.*, p. 666.
[44] *Ibid.*
[45] *Trials of War Criminals*, Doc. 265-PS.

against the Ukrainian partisans in Volynia and Polissya, 50 tanks, 5 armored trains, 27 airplanes, 10 motorized battalions with heavy arms and artillery and nearly 10,000 German and auxiliary police were used. In addition, several Hungarian detachments and Eastern Volunteer battalions participated. During three months of fighting, the Germans lost 3,000 dead, and the Ukrainian side suffered 1,237 insurgents killed, with 5,000 deaths among the Ukrainian civilian population.[46]

The UPA skillfully utilized the assets which it acquired by its independent political position. Special appeals were made by the UPA to different volunteer formations which consisted of former Soviet citizens fighting on the German side. The results of these appeals were spectacular. Early in 1943, a regiment of auxiliary Ukrainian police deserted to the UPA in Volynia.[47] In April, 1943, a battalion of Ukrainian "Schutzmann Police" stationed in Yarmolynci (county of Kamenets-Podilskyi) killed their German officers and marched northward to join the UPA.[48] The nations in parts of Eastern Europe and Asia that fought on the German side could not resist the UPA appeals. The extent of their joining the UPA ranks can be seen from the fact that on the eve of the German retreat from Ukraine, the Ukrainian Insurgent army included 15 different national detachments of such nations as Azerbaijans, Georgians, Tartars, and Cossacks.[49] Encouraged by such successes among the various dominated nations of the East, the UPA convoked the first Conference of the Enslaved Nations of Eastern Europe and Asia. The conference took place Nov. 21-22, 1943, in territory held by UPA. It worked out a program for a common struggle of the oppressed nations against Germany and the USSR. The object of this common struggle—the restoration of the national independence of the nations concerned—was not achieved. But the solidarity shown among the oppressed nations of the Soviet Union by the common struggle for liberation undoubtedly demonstrates the potentialities which could have been successful under more favorable circumstances.

The large-scale anti-German partisan warfare in Ukraine had a considerable impact on the transportation of troops and

[46] Krypyakevych, et al , *op cit.*, p. 672-673
[47] *Ibid.*, p. 660.
[48] *Ibid.*, p. 664.
[49] *Ibid.*, p. 684   See also the Ukrainian Underground paper *To Arms*, Sept 22, 1950, article by O. Logush, Commander Chuprynka on the Conference of the Oppressed Nations.

supplies going to the German Eastern front as well as on the efficiency of the German administration in the occupied area. The trouble caused by the partisans was greatest at the very time when Germany most needed men and supplies to replenish her army in the East after the debacle of Stalingrad. Yet, the supply lines stretched hundreds of miles through a territory containing large-scale partisan bodies. A large part of the new German troops and arms never reached their destination, and a considerable part of them had to be diverted in order to strengthen the German garrisons in Ukraine and to patrol the vital communication lines.

The German retreat from Ukraine was comparatively orderly in the area east of the Dnieper River because the flat and steppe-like terrain there prevented larger partisan actions. The German retreat west of the Dnieper River, which was the main anti-German partisan area of operation, was speedy, chaotic, and marked with many encirclements of their troops and heavy losses.

There is another indication of the impact of Ukrainian partisan warfare on the German armed forces. Early in 1944, most of the voluntary formations organized from Soviet citizens were recalled from the Eastern front and were stationed in Germany and Western Europe. One explanation for this German move was that the reliability of these troops when facing the guerillas was not great and that their possible defection to the side of the independent insurgents was too great a risk for the Germans to take. The German administration, carrying out a systematic exploitation of foods and raw materials, was paralyzed as the result of the large-scale partisan activity. There were difficulties not only in transporting goods to the front or to Germany, but also in obtaining these goods. The German authorities could enforce no systematic deliveries, because they were no longer in control of many villages and regions. Securing food in most areas was possible only through German raids, and these were sporadic and could not produce a sufficient volume to meet the needs of the German army or of the German civilian population. Thus, the predicted partisan movement in Ukraine had a considerable influence on the weakening of the German war effort in the East.

CHAPTER 6

CONCLUSION

Great nations which in the past have created widely and enduring "supranational" conceptions of their roles were able to do so because they had two essential qualifications. The first was rational understanding, which made possible the choice of relevant goals and effective means of policy. The second was the enlistment of their expansive vitality in the service of a strong sense of self-transcendent mission, which provided both a moral justification of and limitation on, the exercise of their will to power. . . . Other imperial powers have failed to achieve wide and enduring acceptance of their system of world order because these systems expressed little more than their egoistic will to power disguised in some overmastering myth rather than enabled and disciplined by a genuine sense of moral mission.[1]

THERE IS LITTLE doubt that the Nazi *Drang nach Osten* was ideological in character and that it was the most essential part of Hitler's expansion policy. In the German expansion toward the East, Ukraine was the most important area to be acquired. It was on Ukraine that the colonization plans of the Third Reich firmly rested. It was obvious to the Nazi leaders that Germany's immediate eastern neighbors—Poland, Czechoslovakia, and the Baltic countries—were too small or too poor in soil for a large scale German land colonization. Ukraine, on the other hand, with 200,000 square miles of the richest land in Europe and possessing abundant raw materials was to Hitler the most desirable colony or, as he envisaged it, a "German India." Just as Great Britain was once willing to fight a series of colonial wars for her dominion and routes to India, Hitler was willing to start a world war in order to obtain his *Lebensraum* in Eastern Europe. But Hitler's plans in the distant steppes of Ukraine were much more sweeping than those

---

[1] William Y. Elliot, *The Political Economy of American Foreign Policy*, (New York: Henry Holt and Co , 1955), p. 386.

pursued by the English in India. He wanted these areas not for a profitable trade, but in terms of "blood and soil." The peasants of German blood were to come to this area and were to cultivate the soil to make it German, all at the expense of the native population which was to be annihilated, enslaved, or expelled.

In German policy can be found one extreme example of the totalitarian imperialism which began after the First World War. It is unprecedented in the history of Western civilization and includes enslavement and extermination of classes, ethnic and religious groups, and even whole nations. Moreover, this was to be accomplished through the use of all means of modern technology and science for the sake of a pseudo-scientific ideology. The totalitarian imperialism is characterized by slave labor camps, concentration camps, and mass graves of innocent victims. These institutions warn us that war itself is not necessarily the worst of evils. Ukraine, during the German invasion in the Second World War, lost about 10,000,000 people; yet relatively few of them died in warfare or circumstances produced by warfare. Most of them were victims of a planned Nazi policy which was designed to prepare the way for a gigantic German colonization. The enslavement and annihilation policy in Eastern Europe would certainly have been intensified after Hitler's victory and a peace on his terms. With the additional power which would have been his, he would have been in a stronger position to have pushed the program of colonization and to have furthered Nazi ideology.

Fortunately, Hitler did not win the war and a defeated Nazi Germany rendered to the Free World her last and only service —a warning of things that might come and of which she was just a forerunner. This warning was echoed in Orwell's visionary novel, *Nineteen Eighty-Four*. Developments in this direction seem likely if the free world should fall again into a state of political apathy, selfishness, colonialism, and easy going peace at any price. It is significant that totalitarian imperialism did grow and is still thriving as a result of the shortcomings and injustices existing in our modern society. Nazi imperialism arose from the injustice of the Versailles Treaty and from the abuses of the horror regime of the Soviet Union in Eastern Europe. Japanese imperialism got its impetus under the slogan "Asia for Asiatics" which tried to exploit the justified anti-colonial feelings of Asiatic peoples against the Western powers. As in the past, the

Soviet Union, which is still an expanding empire, exploits the search for independence by subjugated nations and uses social unrest in any corner of the Free World to her advantage.

The Free World will be able to successfully meet this challenge and to avoid the fate of Ukraine, the Baltic states, and other victims of totalitarian imperialism, if it will use the strength of its society as well as the universality of its ideas. Ideas, not atomic weapons, will be decisive. In the present Cold War between the modern democracies and the totalitarian powers, the formulation and projection of ideas emerges as a primary factor because of the unprecedented risk of an all-out war and because of the growing tendency toward a military and economic deadlock between the competing blocks.

In the course of the Cold War, the totalitarian powers learned that the weakest avenue of the Western defense is its ideology.[2] Consequently, there has been a considerable re-orientation in Soviet foreign policy since the end of 1952. This meant a shift from militant toward a "peaceful" ideological penetration. The new campaign carefully avoids the unpleasant-ness of Marxist-Leninist dogmas such as class struggle, collecti-vism, inevitableness of war, and tries to make its headway by such generally appealing slogans as peace, friendship, progress, and economic, racial, and national emancipation.

The 19th Congress of the Communist Party in 1952, the Pandung Conference in 1954, the Geneva Conference in 1954 to 1955, the Bulganin-Khruschev visit to Asiatic countries in 1955, and the 20th Congress of the Communist Party in 1956 are mile-stones of a gigantic totalitarian "peace" offensive. Though the trend of this offensive is of utmost danger to the Western World, it is too early to judge its ultimate results.

The outcome of this offensive will depend to a great degree on whether the Western World will be able to create a vigorous,

---

[2] As early as 1949, Prof G T. Robinson wrote. "Our principal weakness to-day is not economic or military, but ideological—not a matter of goods or guns, but of ideas . . It is not piecemeal answers that inspire men in 'their finest hour', it is a total conception of the good life . . . In this situation, there is urgent need for philosophic reconstruction and renewal " "The Ideological Combat," *Foreign Affairs,* XXVII, No 4, pp 530-531

Similar findings and conclusions are reflected in Arnold Toynbee's *Civilization on Trial* (1947), W. Y Elliot's *The Political Economy of American Foreign Policy* (1955), H A Kissinger's, "The Limitations of of Diplomacy," *The New Republic,* (May 9, 1955), and in many other articles and books appearing in the Western World in the post-war period They all indicate that the West is not unaware of its weakness on this particular point dynamic, and all embracing ideological response to this challenge and whether it will project this response in time, not only to nations oppressed by Communist totalitarianism but also to many newly emancipated and as yet uncommitted nations of Asia and Africa.

Bibliography

Abshagen, Karl H., *Canaris Patriot und Weltbuerger*, (Stuttgart: Union Deutsche Verlagsgesellschaft, 1950).

Anders, Wladyslaw, *Bez Ostatniego Rozdzialu* [Without the Last Chapter]. Memoirs from years 1939-1946, 2nd ed. (Newton Wales, Montomeryshire: Printing Co., 1950).

Animasov, Oleg, *The German Occupation in the Northern Russia During World War II, Political and Administrative Aspects*, (New York: Research Program on the U.S.S.R., 1954).

Andreyev, V., *Narodnaya Voyna* [The People's War], (Moscow: Gosizdat, 1952).

Armstrong, John A., *Ukrainian Nationalism 1939-1945*, (New York: Columbia University Press, 1955).

Baldwin, Hanson W., *Great Mistakes of the War*, (New York: Harper & Brothers Publishers, 1950).

Beck, Jozef, *Dernier Rapport, Politique Polonaise 1926-1939*, (Neuchatel, Paris: Editions de la Baconniere, 1951).

Bor, Peter, *Gespraeche mit Halder*, (Wiesbaden: Limes Verlag, 1950).

Boyarsky, P. K., *Ukrainska Vnutrishna Polityka OUN* [The Ukrainian Internal Politics of OUN], (Geneva: 1947).

Braeutigam, Otto, *Ueberblick ueber die Besetzten Ostgebiete waehrend des 2. Weltkrieges*, (Tuebingen: Studien des Instituts Besatzungsfragen zu den deutschen Besatzungen im 2. Weltkrieg, 1954).

British War Office, *Who Is Who In Occupied Europe*, (London: 1944).

Bullock, Allen, L.C., *Hitler, A Study in Tyranny*, (London: Ocham Press Ltd., 1952).

Carr, Edward H., *Berlin-Moskau. Deutschland und Russland zwischen den beiden Weltkriegen*, (Stuttgart: Deutsche Verlaganstalt, 1954).

Caulaincourt, Armand, L.S., *With Napoleon in Russia*, (New York: W. Morrow and Co., 1935).

Churchill, Winston, L.S., *The Second World War*, six volumes, (Boston: Published in association with the Cooperation Publishing Co. by Houghton Mifflin Co., 1948-1953).

Ciano, Galeazzo, *The Ciano Diaries 1939-1943*, (Garden City, N.Y.: Doubleday & Co., Inc., 1946).

Coates, K. and W. P. Zelda, *History of Anglo-Soviet Relations*, (London: Lawrence & Wishart, 1944).

Coole, W. W. and M. F. Potter, *Thus Speaks Germany*, (New York: Harper & Brothers Publishers, 1941).

Czapsky, Joseph, *The Inhuman World*, (New York: Sheed & Ward, Inc., 1952).

Dixon, Aubry, C. Brigadier, and Otto Heilbrunn: *Communist Guerilla Warfare*, (London: George Allen & Unwin Ltd., 1954).

Dvinov, B., *Vlasovskoye Dvizheniye v Svetle Dokumentov* [Vlassov Movement in the Light of Documents], (New York: 1950).

Elliot, William Y., et al., *The Political Economy of American Foreign Policy, Its Concepts, Strategy, and Limits*. Report of a Study Group sponsored by the Woodrow Wilson Foundation and the National Planning Association, (New York: Henry Holt and Co., 1955). ·

Encyclopediya Ukrainoznavstva [Encyclopedia of Ukraine], (New York and Munich: Shevchenko Scientific Society, 1949).

Eisenhower, Dwight D., *Crusade in Europe*, (Garden City, N.Y.: Doubleday & Co., Inc., 1952).

Foerster, Friedrich W., *Europe and the German Question*, (New York: Sheed & Ward, Inc., 1940).

Fuller, J. F. C., *The Second World War 1939-1945*, (New York: Sloan and Pearce, 1949).

Gafencu, Grigore, *Prelude to the Russian Campaign, from the Moscow Pact (Aug. 21, 1939) to the Opening Hostilities in Russia (June 22, 1941)*, (London: F. Muller Ltd., 1945).

Geyer, C., *Hitler's New Order*, (London: Hutchison & Co., Ltd., 1942).

Gilbert, Felix, *Hitler Directs His War*, (New York: Oxford University Press, 1951).

Goerlitz, Walter, *Der Zweite Weltkrieg, 1939-1945*, (Stuttgart: Steingrueben Verlag, 1951).

Goerlitz, Walter, and Quint, Herbert A., *Adolpf Hitler (Eine Biographie)*, (Stuttgart: Steingrueben Verlag, 1952).

Guderian, Gen. Heinz, *Panzer Leader*, (New York: E. P. Dutton & Co., 1952).

Halder, Franz, *Hitler als Feldherr*, (Munich: Dom-Verlag, 1949).

Hitler, Adolf, *Mein Kampf*. Trans. by Ralph Manheim. (New York: Literary Classics, Inc., 1943, distributed by Houghton Mifflin Co., Boston).

Holldack, Heinz, *Was Wirklich Geschah. Die diplomatischen Hintergruende der deutschen Kriegspolitik*, (Munich: Nymphenburger Verlagshandlung, 1949)

Ignatov, B., *Zapysky Partizana* [Diary of a Partisan], (Moscow: Gosizdat, 1951).

Ilnytzkyj, Roman, *Deutschland und die Ukraine 1939-1945, Tatsachen europaeischer Ostpolitik*. Ein Vorbericht, Erster Band, 1. Buch, (Munich: Osteuropa Institut, 1955).

Karov, D., *Partyzanskoye Dvizheniye v SSSR v 1941-1945*, [The Partisan Movement in the USSR in 1941-1945], (Munich: Institute for the Study of the History and Culture of the USSR, 1954).

Kern, Erich, *Der Grosse Rausch, Russland Feldzug 1941-1945*, (Zuerich: Thomas Verlag, 1950).

Kleist, Peter, *Auch Du Warst Dabei, Ein Buch des Aergnissess und der Hoffnung*, (Heidelberg: K. Vowinckel, 1952).

Kleist, Peter, *Zwischen Hitler und Stalin 1939-1945*, (Bonn: Athenaeum Verlag, 1950).

Knoop, Walter, *Die Politische Aufgabe der Gegenwart*, 2nd ed., (Leipzig: Der Nationale Aufbau Verlag, Guenther Heining, 1944).

Kolinov, Kyrill D., *Die Sowjetmarschaelle Haben das Wort*, (Hamburg: Hanse Verlag, 1950).

Kovpak, S. A., *Ot Putyvla do Karpat* [From Putvyl to the Carpathian Mountains], (Moscow-Leningrad: Gospolitizdat, 1945).

Kordt, Erich, *Wahn und Wirklichkeit*, (Stuttgart: Union Deutsche Verlagsgesellschaft, 1948).

Kozlov, I. W., *V Krymskom Podpolyu* [In the Crimean Underground], (Moscow: Sovyetsky Pisatel, 1952).

Krypyakevych, Ivan, et al., *Istoriya Ukrainskoho Viyska* [The History of the Ukrainian Armed Forces], ed. by Myron Levytsky, 2nd rev. ed., (Winnipeg: Ukrainian Book Club, Ltd., 1953).

Kubiyovych, Volodymyr, *Istoriya Ukrainskoho Centralnoho Komitetu v Heneralniy Huberniyi* [The History of the Ukrainian Central Committee in the General Government]. Unpublished typed manuscript located in the Archive of the Osteuropa Institute, Munich.

Lewin, Percy E., *The German Road to the East*, (London: Williams Heineman, 1917).

Londonderry, the Marquis of, *Ourselves and Germany*, (London: R. Hall, Ltd., 1938).

Lemkin, Rafal, *Axis Rule in Occupied Europe, Laws of occupation, analysis of government, proposals for redress.* (Washington: Carnegie Endowment for International Peace, Division of International Law, 1944).

Lukacs, John A., *The Great Powers & Eastern Europe*, (New York: American Book Co., 1953).

Manning, Clarence, *Twentieth Century Ukraine*, (New York: Bookmen Associates, Inc., 1951).

Machiavelli, N., *The Prince.* Trans. by N. H. Thomson, (Oxford: Clarendon Press, 1917).

Matla, Zynoviy, *Pivdenna Pokhidna Hrupa* [The Southern Task Force], (Munich: Cicero, 1952).

Medvedyev, D., *Sylnyye Dukhom* [Those of Strong Spirit], (Moscow: Voyennoye izdat., 1951).

Meier-Benneken, Paul, *Das Dritte Reich im Aufbau*, (Berlin: Junker und Duennhaupt Verlag, 1946).

Meinecke, Friedrich, *Die Deutsche Katastrophe*, (Wiesbaden: Eberhard Brockhaus Verlag, 1946).

Mikolajczyk, Stanislaw, *The Pattern of Soviet Domination*, (London: Sampson Low, Marston, 1948).

Mirchuk, Petro, *Ukrayinska Povstancha Armiya* [The Ukrainian Insurgent Army], (Munich: Cicero, 1953).

Moltke, Kai, *Bag Kulisserne; imperialismens aggression omkring og under den unden verdenskrieg* [Behind the Backstage of the Second World War], (Kopenhavn: Vorlaget Tiden, 1951).

Moore, B., Jr., *Terror and Progress USSR*, (Cambridge: Harvard University Press, 1954).

Mowat, Charles L., *Britain Between the Wars 1918-1940*, (Bristol: The University of Chicago Press, 1955).

Mussolini, Benito, *Memoirs: 1942-1943*, (London: Weidenfeld & Nicolson, 1949).

Namier, Lewis, Bernstein, *Diplomatic Prelude, 1938-1939*, (London: Macmillan, 1948).

Namier, Lewis, Bernstein, *Europe in Decay, A Study in disintegration, 1936-1940*, (London: Macmillan, 1950).

Namier, Lewis, Bernstein, *Facing East*, (New York: Harper, 1948).

Oberkommando der Wehrmacht, *Kampf gegen die Sowjets, Berichte und Bilder vom Beginn des Ostfeldzuges bis zum Fruehjahr 1942*, (Berlin: Zeitgeschichte Verlag, 1943).

Oehquist, J. W., *Das Reich des Fuehrers*, (Bonn: L. Rohrscheid, 1941).

OUN v Viyni [The OUN in War], Information Section of the OUN, (April, 1946).

Papen, Franz von, *Memoirs*, (New York: E. P. Dutton & Co., 1953).

Picker, Henry, Dr., *Hitler's Tischgeschpraeche, im Fuehrerhauquartier, 1941-1942*, (Bonn: Athenaeum Verlag, 1951).

Polikarpenko, H., *Orhanizatsiya Ukrains'kykh Natsionalistiv pidchas Druhoyi Svitovoyi Viyny* [The Organization of the Ukrainian Nationalists during the Second World War], ed. by B. Mykhaylyuk, 4th rev. ed., (Canada: OUN v Viyni, 1951).

Polskie Sily Zbrojne w Drugiej Wojnie Swiatowej, Vol. 3, *Armija Krajowa* [Polish Armed Forces During W.W. II, Vol. 3, Home Army], (London: Instytut im. Gen. Sikorskiego, Krajowa, 1950).

Price, Morgan P., *Hitler's War and Eastern Europe*, (London: G. Allen and Unwin, Ltd., 1940).

Rauschnig, Herman, *Gespraeche mit Hitler*, (New York: Europa Verlag, 1940).

Rosenberg, Alfred, *Kampf um die Macht*. Ed. by Rhilo von Trotha, successor of F. Eher, (Munich: Trotha, 1937).

Rosenberg, Alfred, *Das Mythos des 20 Jahrhunderts, Eine Wertung der Seelischgeistigen Gestaltungskaempfe Unserer Zeit*, (Munich: Hoheneichen-Verlag, 1943).

Rosenberg, Alfred, *Der Welt Kampf und die Weltrevolution Unserer Zeit, Rede von Reichsleiter und Reichsminister Rosenberg auf der 2. Tagung der Union Nationaler Journalisten Verbaende, Vienna, June 22, 1943*, (Munich: F. Eher Nachf., 1943).

Rossi, A., *The Russo-German Alliance, August 1939-June 1941*, (Boston: The Beacon Press, 1951).

Samarin, Vladimir, D., *Civilian Life under the German Occupation*, (New York: Research Program on the U.S.S.R., 1954).

Schmidt, Dr. Paul, *Hitler's Interpreter*, (London: Heinmann, 1951).

Schmidt, Dr. Paul, *Statist auf Diplomatischer Buehne*, (Bonn: Athenaeum Verlag, 1949).

Schuman, Frederick L., *International Politics*, 4th ed., (New York: McGraw-Hill Book Co., 1948).

Smal-Stocki, Roman, *The Nationality Problem of the Soviet Union and Russian Communist Imperialism*, (Milwaukee: Bruce Publishing Co., 1952).

Snyder, Louis L., *From Bismarck to Hitler, Background of Modern German Nationalism*, (Williamsport: Bayard Press, 1935).

Stipp, John L., *Devils Diary, The Record of Nazi Conspiracy and Aggression*, (Yellow Springs, Ohio: The Antioch Press, 1955).

Stukalich, Iuriy, *Vtoraya Mirovaya Voyna v Byelorussiyi* [The Second World War in Byelo-Russia], (New York: Research Program on the U.S.S.R., 1953).

Tannenberg, Otto R., *Grossdeutschland, Die Arbeit des 20 Jahrhundert*, (Leipzig-Gehlis: B. Volger, 1911).

Thorwald, Juergen, *Wen Sie Verderben Wollen*, (Suttgart: Steingrueben Verlag, 1952).

Tippelskirch, Kurt von, *Geschichte des Zweiten Weltkrieges*, (Bonn: Athenaeum Verlag, 1951).

Toynbee, Arnold, *Survey of International Affairs 1939-1946*, Vol. 4, *Hitler's Europe*, (London: Oxford University Press, 1954).

U.S.A. State Department: *Nazi-Soviet Relations 1939-1941*, (Washington, D.C.,: Government Printing Office, 1948).

Vershygora, P., *Ludy z Chystoy Sovestyu* [The People With an Unstrained Conscience], (Moscow: Sovetsky Pisatel, 1951).

Virski, Fred, *My Life in the Red Army*, (New York: The Macmillan Co., 1949).

Waite, R. G. L., *Vanguard of Nazism, The Free Corps, 1918-1923*, (Cambridge, Mass.: Harvard University Press, 1952).

War Department, *The World at War, 1939-1944*, (Washington: The Infantry Journal, 1945).

Weigert, Hans W., *German Geopolitics*, (New York: Oxford University Press, 1941).

Weigert, Hans, *Generals and Geographers, The Twilight of Geopolitics*, (London: Oxford University Press, 1942).

Weinberg, Gerhardt, *Germany and the Soviet Union, 1939-1941*, (Leiden: E. J. Brill, 1954).

Wilmot, Chester, *The Struggle for Europe*, (New York: Harper & Brothers Publishers, 1952).

ARTICLES

Gurian, Waldemar, "The Philosophy of the Totalitarian State," in Charles Hart, *Philosophy of the State*, 1940.

Machray, Robert, "Hitler's Trail over Europe," *The Fortnightly Review*, (June, 1934).

Mayer, Henry C., "Germans in the Ukraine, 1918," *The American Slavic and East European Review*, (April, 1950).

Mykhalchuk, V., "Korotkyi Narys do Chervonoyi Armiyi," [Short Introduction to the Studies of the Red Army], *Rozbudova Derzavy* [Development of State], (Autumn, 1954).

Lawton, Lancelot, "The Oppressed Ukrainians," *The Fortnightly Review*, (April, 1934).

Lawton, Lancelot, "Ukrainian Europe's Greatest Problem," *East Europe and Contemporary Russia*, Vol. 3, No. 1, (Spring, 1939).

Robinson, G. T., "The Ideological Combat," *Foreign Affairs*, Vol. 27, No. 4.

Snow, Edgar, "The Ukraine Pays the Bill," *Saturday Evening Post*, (Jan. 27, 1945).

Stercho, P. (translator), "Konferenciya Hitlera z Feldmarshalom Keitlem i Generalom Zeitzlerom v Berghofi" [Hitler's Conference with the Fieldmarshal Keitel and General Zeitzler in the Berghof], *Rozbudova Derzavy* [Development of State], (Summer, 1954).

Shandruk, P., "It Was This Way," in *Development of State*, No. 3 (14), (Autumn, 1954).

Thayer, Charles W., "Can Russia Trust Her 'Slave Armies'?" *Saturday Evening Post*, (Aug. 7, 1954).

Vogel, George, "Hitler's Krieg gegen England," *Europa Archiv*, (Sept. 5, 1954).

Weer, Hans De, "Erich Koch and Ukraine," *The Ukrainian Quarterly*, Vol. XI, No. 1, (Winter, 1955).

DOCUMENTS

Amtliches Material zum Massenmord von Winniza, (Berlin, Zentral Verlag der NSDAP, 1944).

Documents on British Foreign Policy, 1919-1939, Third Series, Vol. IV, (London: H. M. Stationary Office, 1941).

Documents on German Foreign Policy, 1918-1945, Ser. D. Vols. IV and V, (Washington, D.C.: U.S. Government Printing Office, 1953).

Documents and Materials Relating to the Eve of the Second World War, Vols. I and II, (New York: International Publishers, 1948).

Himmler's File in Drawer No. 7, Folder No. 252, *Reports on the Resistance Movements in Eastern Europe,* (Hoover Library Collection).

International Military Tribunal, *Trial of the Major War Criminals,* Vols. I to XXXXII, (Nuremberg, Secretariat of the Tribunal, 1943).

Der Kampf Gegen den Westen 1940, Documents and articles collected by Dr. Hans Volz, (Berlin, Junker und Duennhaupt Verlag, 1943).

Military Court of the Supreme Court of the U.S.S.R., *Sprawozdanie Sadowe w Sprawie Organizatorow, Kierownikow i Uczestmikow Polskiego Podziemia w Zapleczu Armiji Czerwonej na Terytorium Polski, Litwy, oraz Obwodow Zachodnich Bialorusi i Ukrainy* [Court Records of the Instigators, Leaders and Participants of the Polish Underground in the Hinterland of the Red Army on the Territory of Poland, Lithuania, and in the Western Provinces of Byelo-Russia and Ukraine], (Moscow: The Peoples Commissariat of Justice, 1945).

Trials of War Criminals Before the Nueremberg Military Tribunals Under Council Law No. 10, Vols. 1 to 14, (Washington, D.C.: U.S. Government Printing Office, 1949).

Wneshnaya Politika Sovetskovo Souyuza u Period Otchestwennoy Woyny, Dokumenty i materialy [The Interior Policy of the Soviet Union During the Period of the Fatherland War, Documents and Materials], Vols. I and II, (Moscow: Ogiz, 1946).

PERIODICALS

Deutsche Bug-Zeitung. Amtsblatt des Generalkommissars fuer den Generalbezirk Nikolajew. Nikolayev, semi - weekly, (March, 1942-January, 1944), in the Library of Congress.

Der Deutsche in Transnistrien. Odessa, weekly, (July 1942-January 1944), in the Library of Congress.

Deutsche Ukraine Zeitung. Lutsk daily, (January 1942-January 1944), in the Library of Congress.

Krakauer Zeitung. Cracow daily, (November, 1939-February, 1945) in the Library of Congress.

Wschod—organ sluzacy sprawie polskiej na Ziemiach Wschodnich East [periodical promoting the Polish cause in the Eastern provinces]. Issues from June 22, 1943, and Feb. 18, 1944, in the Hoover Library, Stanford.

Index

CPSIA information can be obtained at www.ICGtesting.com
Printed in the USA
BVOW07s2242030615

403179BV00014B/85/P